A Pragmatic Guide to
Business Process Modelling

The British Computer Society

The British Computer Society is the leading professional body for the IT industry. With members in over 100 countries, the BCS is the professional and learned Society in the field of computers and information systems.

The BCS is responsible for setting standards for the IT profession. It is also leading the change in public perception and appreciation of the economic and social importance of professionally managed IT projects and programmes. In this capacity, the Society advises, informs and persuades industry and government on successful IT implementation.

IT is affecting every part of our lives and that is why the BCS is determined to promote IT as *the* profession of the 21st century.

Joining the BCS

BCS qualifications, products and services are designed with your career plans in mind. We not only provide essential recognition through professional qualifications but also offer many other useful benefits to our members at every level.

Membership of the BCS demonstrates your commitment to professional development. It helps to set you apart from other IT practitioners and provides industry recognition of your skills and experience. Employers and customers increasingly require proof of professional qualifications and competence. Professional membership confirms your competence and integrity and sets an independent standard that people can trust. www.bcs.org/membership

Further Information

Further information about the British Computer Society can be obtained from: The British Computer Society, 1 Sanford Street, Swindon, Wiltshire, SN1 1HJ, UK.
Telephone: + 44 (0)1793 417 424
Email: bcs@hq.bcs.org.uk
Web: www.bcs.org

A Pragmatic Guide to Business Process Modelling

Jon Holt

THE BRITISH COMPUTER SOCIETY

The British Computer Society,
1 Sanford Street,
Swindon, Wiltshire SN1 1HJ,
UK
www.bcs.org

ISBN 1-902505-66-2

British Cataloguing in Publication Data.
A CIP catalogue record for this book is available at the British Library.

Typeset by Tradespools, Frome, Somerset.
Printed at Antony Rowe Ltd., Chippenham, Wiltshire.

This book is dedicated to my beautiful bride-to-be, Rebecca

Contents

Figures

Author

Jon Holt obtained his PhD from University of Wales Swansea in 1991 in the field of real-time systems modelling. Since then, he has worked extensively in the application of modelling to all aspects of systems, including: requirements, process modelling, architectural modelling and educational systems. Jon is the Managing Director and founder of Brass Bullet Ltd, a consultancy and training company based in Swansea, UK. He is an active consultant and has worked in many industries, ranging from engineering to government to schools.

Jon also holds positions at several universities, both in the UK and the US.

He currently lives in Swansea, with his family and evil cat. His outside interests include Tae Kwon Do and card magic.

Foreword

Organizational design is one of the biggest challenges facing business in the 21st century. In the knowledge economy, the ability of the human intellect to solve problems and add value is the key source of competitive advantage. But most of the organizational structures in existence today were designed to add value through the processing of physical assets by labour. So how do you organize for success when your primary resources are intangible? How do you unleash the potential of knowledge workers to transform ideas into value? With so many mutations of organizational forms into networks, communities and collaborative ventures what will the organizational forms of the future look like? No one can be sure of the answers to these questions. But one thing is certain. Whatever the structures and forms of the organizations of the future, people will come together as stakeholders to apply their minds and efforts to the transformation of assets. In other words, they will take part in business processes.

The organizations of the future will face increasing complexity in the external environment. The speed of change will continue to increase as global markets open up all value propositions to ever faster cycles of innovation and imitation, fuelling fast, effective and aggressive competition. Demands on organization from stakeholders will also build. Sometimes it will be expressed through regulators; sometimes through more direct channels. Faced with this growing external complexity, organizations will require highly evolved internal and inter-organizational processes to cope with managing and balancing these multiple demands in transparent, effective and systemic ways. Achieving this will require a language that is up to the task and a discipline that has proven value.

Until recently the languages available for modelling processes were rather inadequate for this task. Neither was there a systematic discipline or approach that promised much. As a result, business process modelling has, to date, greatly underachieved its potential. The ground was ripe for an innovation. In Jon Holt's first book, *UML for Systems Engineering*, he delivered that innovation by taking a language forged in the rigours of software development and opening our eyes to the potential of this language in a creative yet robust modelling approach. A lot of good work followed this innovation and the modelling approach has since been applied to processes as diverse as fishing, taxation, and the management of biodiversity.

In this new volume, Jon builds on this experienced success and takes us further into a modelling approach that should have broad appeal to those with a stake in business processes. The book is a lesson in good practice on business process modelling with relevance to important areas such as risk management, dealing with complexity and the modelling and application of key business standards. Jon's clear and engaging style makes a potentially difficult subject highly accessible and the reader's progress is helped along by the mixture of good examples, humour and flair for explanation that we have come to expect from this author. A book that demonstrates what can be achieved with business process modelling would have been welcome in itself, but a book like this that teaches, inspires and gives real insight into the field will be a valuable catalyst for modelling businesses in all sectors and geographies.

Paul McNeillis MBA, PhD, MCIM
Head of Professional Services, BSI

Acknowledgements

As with everything in life, this project has not been carried out in isolation but is the result of work carried out over the last ten years. Therefore, it would be impossible to mention all the people who have contributed to this book either directly or indirectly. However, having said that, there are a few people who deserve particular note and merit.

First and foremost, all my co-workers at Brass Bullet Ltd, in particular Ian, Simon, Guy and Sylvia. Kay deserves a special mention for being my non-technical guinea pig during the proofreading stages.

In terms of our clients and friends, particular thanks goes to Paul MacNeillis and all his staff, who are far too numerous and fluid to mention – besides, it will only go to their heads and I can't spell any of their names. Other people who deserve credit are Bryan (have a happy retirement), Duncan Disorderly and the rest of their merry crew; Richard Barrow from RSSB and Jeff, for getting us there in the first place; Nigel Fry of the BBC and his staff; the IEE (probably heresy in a BCS book), the systems engineering professional network, and many, many more. If I have missed you off, drop me an email and I'll put you in the second edition.

Thanks should also be directed to the good folk of the BCS who have all helped in the development of this book, including Matthew Flynn, Suzannah Marsh, Elaine Boyes, Sarah Price and Shena Deuchars.

Of course my eternal gratitude goes out to both Mike and Sue Rodd – Mike being the 'Yoda' to my 'Obi Wan'.

Finally, and by no means least, my unconditional love and thanks go to my family: Rebecca, Jude, Eliza and baby Roo, who continue to inspire me in everything I do.

Abbreviations

BPMI	Business Process Modelling Initiative
BPML	Business Process Modelling Language
BSI	British Standards Institution
CMM	capability maturity model
CMMI	capability maturity model integrated
CORBA	Common Object Request Broker Architecture
eGIF	Electronic Government Interoperability Framework
EMC	electro-magnetic compatibility
EN	European Normative
ESA	European Space Agency
HMRI	Her Majesty's Railway Inspectorate
HSE	Health and Safety Executive
IEC	International Electrotechnical Commission
ISO	International Standardization Organization
PGI	process group index
PGR	process group ratio
PI	process index
PMI	process model index
PR	process ratio
RACI	responsible, accountable, consulted and informed
UML	Unified Modelling Language

Glossary

Activity The behavioural steps involved in a process that produce and consume artefacts and that are owned by stakeholders.

Artefact Anything that is produced or consumed by a process or activity.

Assessment A review of a process that is based on a standard. Assessments may be formal or informal and carried out either internally or externally to the organization.

Audit A formal review of a process based on a standard. Audits are carried out by independent, third-party auditors.

Business process management The coordination and management of a business process which will, invariably, involve some sort of business process modelling.

Business process modelling Any process modelling exercise that is performed in order to enhance the overall operation of a business.

Business process re-engineering Used specifically when business process modelling is applied to existing processes as part of a process improvement exercise.

Class Used as template for something and usually a noun. For example, the class 'Person' would represent all people generally, rather than a specific person. Classes are represented graphically by rectangles and can be further described by identifying attributes and operations. Classes form the basic nodes in the class diagram.

Hazard Anything that occurs that can lead to a risk. The terms 'hazard' and 'risk' are often confused, but there are subtle differences between them. It is possible for many hazards to lead to the same risk. For example, there is a risk in a hospital that a power failure will lead to many problems, perhaps even endangering the lives of some patients. There are, however, many hazards that may lead to this risk manifesting itself, such as: a lightening strike, terrorist action, not paying the utility bill, lack of maintenance, and so on.

Instance A specific item within a class. A specific person, for example, Fred Smith, would be an instance within the class 'Person'.

Iteration A self-contained set of process executions within a process. For example, different teams working on the same project will have their own iterations within the same process.

Model This book uses the classic UML definition of a model, which is 'a simplification of reality'. In this way, a model may be an equation, a diagram, a physical model, a piece of text or any verbal description.

Operation Usually represented by a verb that signifies something that a class does.

Operations management Often used in the context of business and management courses and, although it has a wider scope than just process modelling, contains, and relies very heavily upon, process modelling.

Process An approach to doing something that consists of a number of activities, each of which will produce and/or consume some sort of artefact. Each of these activities is the responsibility of a single stakeholder role.

Process group A container for processes that is defined based on functionality of processes, rather than phases in a life cycle. Process groups are often abstract.

Process mapping Refers to relating different processes to one another and forms an integral part of any audit or assessment exercise. Of course, in order to map effectively, all processes must be modelled in some way.

Process meta-model A meta-model is a model of a model, and the process meta-model is a model of a model that is used for process modelling.

Process re-alignment Often applied to existing processes that have, over a period of time, gone out of date for some reason – usually because the requirements for the process have changed and the process is no longer fit for its original purpose.

Relationship Represents the identification of a conceptual relationship between one or more classes. A relationship is represented graphically by variations on a line, depending on the type of relationship. There are four types of relationship used for process modelling: the association, the aggregation, the generalization/specialization and the dependency. Relationships form the basic paths in the class diagram.

Risk A product of the likelihood, or probability, of the risk occurring and the effect of the hazard. In many scenarios, risk is defined by a simple mathematical formula, where *risk = probability × severity*, or it is defined in terms of a simple matrix that has one axis defining the likelihood in words and the other axis defining the severity of the outcome.

Role Part played by a person, place or thing that has an interest in the system or project. The term is often used interchangeably with the term 'stakeholder role'.

Stakeholder Refers to the *role* played by a person, place or thing that has some sort of interest in the system or project. Stakeholders should not be confused with people, as it is possible for a single person to have more than one stakeholder role and, conversely, it is possible for a single stakeholder role to have a number of individuals' names against it. Stakeholders are often not actually people, but the roles of organizations, the environment, places, things, and so on.

Stereotype A way of tailoring the UML language for a particular application.

System Any entity or collection of entities that collaborate in some way to meet a set of requirements. In this way, a system can be a person, a group of people, a family, a computer, a network of computers, mechanics, electronics or just about anything else.

Swim lane An area on an activity with a defined border, the contents of which are associated with a stakeholder. The stakeholder is then responsible for all activities within the swim lane.

UML meta-model A UML model of the UML. This term is fully defined in the UML standard (see www.omg.org).

Validation Refers to something that meets its original requirements or, to put it another way, that does what it's supposed to do. In order to understand validation, the question 'am I building the correct system?' may be asked. It is possible and, indeed, not uncommon for a system to be built that works but that does not meet the original requirements, which makes the system useless.

Verification Refers to something that works correctly and without error. For example, this could be a system that has been tested and runs in an error-free fashion. In order to understand verification, the question , 'am I building the system correctly?' may be asked.

Useful Websites

www.bcs.org
The website of the British Computer Society, which provides useful information and from which you can purchase books on subjects related to process modelling.

www.bpmi.org
The website of the Business Process Management Initiative.

www.bsi-global.org
The website for the British Standards Institution, where standards may be purchased and from which there are links to other standards sites.

www.govtalk.gov.uk
The website of the UK Cabinet Office, which provides information on policies and standards for e-government.

www.iso.org/iso/en/ISOOnline.frontpage
The website of the International Organization for Standardization, from which you can order copies of the ISO standards referenced in this book.

www.omg.org
The Object Management Group website, from which you can download the original UML standard.

www.sei.cmu.edu/cmmi
Information about CMMI provided by the Software Engineering Institute.

www.software.org/quagmire
The Systems and Software Consortium software quagmire.

Preface

Processes form the heart of any organization, regardless of its size, type or age. Any organization that actually does anything will, whether it realizes or not, follow processes. These processes may be formal, documented processes or may be informal processes that exist only inside people's heads. Regardless of the nature of the processes, they will all exhibit three features: they will be complex, require a deep level of understanding and will need to be communicated. This is where the modelling fits in.

The process modelling approach adopted in this book is based on the most popular and widely used modelling language in the world – the UML (Unified Modelling Language), which was created as an open standard and is now an ISO standard.

The approach detailed in this book is the result of ten years of definition, refinement and application of such modelling techniques to all aspects of process modelling and to all types of process. This approach has been implemented in many fields, including: defence, government departments, transport, manufacturing, finance, food, IT, communications, education, aerospace and many more.

Process modelling is by no means a simple task and, therefore, to approach such a project requires the use of appropriate and powerful tools. The approach in this book provides a set of 'sharp tools' that may be employed in any process initiative.

1 Introduction

'Process and procedure are the last hiding place for people who don't have the wit or wisdom to do their jobs properly.'

David Brent, *The Office*, BBC

THE MAGIC OF PROCESSES

Processes are an integral part of everyday life. Every time we, as human beings, perform any kind of action, we are actually carrying out a process. This may vary from the way that we get dressed each morning, the way we cross the street on the way to work, to the way that we cook our food in the evenings. The key word used here is 'way' as, in essence, a process simply describes the way to do something or, to put it another way, an 'approach'. It is possible to identify and relate processes for every single action that we take in life. However, this would clearly be a very large number, if not infinity!

Using processes effectively, however, is often not quite so straightforward. There is a big difference between observing a process and performing a process effectively. Consider the example of a magic trick being performed by a magician who is, quite clearly, following some sort of predefined process. It is easy to watch and follow a magic trick, such as a card trick. The magician shuffles the cards and asks a member of the audience to choose one. The audience member selects the card, memorizes it, shows it to the rest of the audience and then places back into the pack. The deck is then shuffled. After a few clever words and a bit of showmanship, the card reappears underneath a vase, or in a pocket or on the other side of the room. The crowd are impressed and give their applause, much to the pleasure of the magician.

A trick such as this is one that everyone can follow and appreciate, but one that most people cannot actually perform themselves. In fact, it is possible for someone to follow the *exact* steps that were carried out by the magician, but to fail utterly in producing the chosen card. There are a number of possible reasons for this:

- The layman, when trying to perform the trick, simply does not understand what has actually gone on. There is a big difference between what is perceived by an observer and what actually occurs. Invariably, this is deliberate on behalf of the magician but something that can be quite clear to a fellow magician who has the relevant domain knowledge. Such trickery may involve a deck that is arranged into a particular order, the use of false cards or the pre-placing of copies of cards around a room.

- The trick itself is far more complex than it first appears. There are subtleties and nuances of the activities carried out by the magician – false cuts, double lifts, palmed cards and the like. The deception is not just limited to the cards themselves, but may also include sneaking looks at various cards, distracting the attention of the audience by waving the hands or orally catching people's attention. All of these activities are designed to look like natural actions to a casual observer.

- The information conveyed by the magician is not the true reality of what has actually happened. Deliberate distractions and misdirection techniques can be employed to send the wrong information to the audience.

The effective manipulation of processes is very much like the manipulation of playing cards, albeit without the deliberate intention to mislead. To capture a process is very often not as simple as just watching somebody perform a task and then copying the perceived actions. Without a good knowledge of what is actually going on, this task can be very difficult. If the process is not captured effectively and accurately, then it will be impossible to reproduce the results of the process. There are a number of ways to ensure that the process is captured correctly:

- The trick must be looked at from several points of view, rather than purely from the point of view of a casual observer. In fact, with a rigorous and structured approach to observing what is going on from a number of different perspectives, almost any trick can be worked out to some degree.

- The end result must be related back to the initial conditions of the trick and full traceability established. How is it possible to go from one set of conditions to another – if it does not seem possible then there is some key information missing.

- The role of all the participants must be examined, including the audience members and the magician. But it is not good enough to stop there, as there may be several other roles that exist that are not obvious – what about the possibility of the magician having an accomplice either in the audience or on the other end of a phone line or radio line? These are techniques that are regularly employed by magicians.

- Finally, and perhaps most importantly, it is essential to understand what the overall intention of the trick is and what effect it will have on the audience.

The intention of this book is to help you to master the magic of processes. It will increase your understanding of processes, enable you to control complexity and to communicate your ideas effectively. This is achieved by identifying a number of 'views' that are required in order to model a process completely and fully. Seven views are identified and each one is described in detail.

BACKGROUND

It is not just people that follow processes, as every organization in existence, whether it is a single-person company or a multinational organization, will rely on a number of processes to function effectively. Depending on the size of the organization and the complexity of its set up, the number of processes that a company uses can be huge – almost infinite, again.

Process modelling is arguably one of the most important aspects of any organization in terms of the management and control of all of the organizational activities. These activities will range from the high-level business activities, including mission statements, business processes and requirements, right down to very detailed technical processes that may be executed on a daily basis within the organization.

Business process modelling goes under many different names and labels so, in order to keep things simple, the term *process modelling* in this book may be replaced by any of the following terms:

- **Business process modelling**: any process modelling exercise that is performed in order to enhance the overall operation of a business.

- **Business process management**: the coordination and management of a business process which will, invariably, involve some sort of business process modelling.

- **Business process re-engineering**: used specifically when business process modelling is applied to existing processes as part of a process improvement exercise.

- **Operations management**: often used in the context of business and management courses and, although it has a wider scope than just process modelling, it contains and relies very heavily upon process modelling.

- **Process mapping**: refers to relating different processes to one another and forms an integral part of any audit or assessment exercise. Of course, in order to map effectively, all processes must be modelled in some way.

- **Process re-alignment**: often applied to existing processes that have, over a period of time, gone out of date for some reason – usually because the requirements for the process have changed and the process is no longer fit for its original purpose.

This book covers all of the above definitions at various points but, as should be clear from this list, all of these different concepts rely heavily on the fact that processes can be modelled in some way. As the book focuses on business process modelling, the modelling techniques can be applied to any or all of the above areas.

SOME BASIC DEFINITIONS

This section presents some definitions for the basic terminology that is used in this book.

- **Process**: although a term that is very widely used, the term 'process' is also one that, depending on the source, has many different interpretations. The following list contains just a few definitions:

  - a series of actions, changes, or functions bringing about a result (*Oxford English Dictionary*, 2002);

  - a series of operations performed in the making or treatment of a product (*Oxford English Dictionary*, 2002);

  - a set of interrelated activities, which transforms inputs into outputs (ISO/IEC 15504, 2004).

For the purposes of this book, a process is simply *an approach to doing something that consists of a number of activities, each of which will produce and/or consume some sort of artefact. Each of these activities is the responsibility of a single stakeholder role.*

There are many types of process that are defined, such as operational processes, business processes, technical processes, natural processes, biological processes, political processes, financial processes, and so on. For the purposes of this book, the term 'process' may be applied equally to any or all of these types of process.

- **System**: any entity or collection of entities that collaborate in some way to meet a set of requirements. In this way, a system can be a person, a group of people, a family, a computer, a network of computers, mechanics, electronics and just about anything else.

- **Artefact**: defined as anything that is produced or consumed by a process or activity.

- **Stakeholder**: refers to the *role* played by a person, place or thing that has some sort of interest in the system or project. Stakeholders should not be confused with people, as it is possible for a single person to have more than one stakeholder role and, conversely, it is possible for a single stakeholder role to have a number of individuals' names against it. Indeed, stakeholders are often not actually people, but the roles of organizations, the environment, places, things, and so on.

- **Model**: in this book, the definition of 'model' is taken from the classic UML (Unified Modelling Language) definition, which is 'a simplification of reality'. In this way, a model may be an equation, a diagram, a physical model, a piece of text or any verbal description.

- **Verification**: refers to something that works correctly and without error. For example, this could be a system that has been tested and runs in an error-free fashion. In order to understand verification, the question 'am I building the system correctly?' may be asked.

- **Validation**: refers to something that meets its original requirements or, to put it another way, that does what it is supposed to do. In order to understand validation, the question 'am I building the correct system?' may be asked. It is possible and, indeed, not uncommon for a system to be built that works but that does not meet the original requirements, which makes it useless!

Some of these terms will be redefined at other points in this book, as they are so fundamental and important to understanding process modelling, that they can never be defined too often.

RISK

Risk is something that affects every person, every day of their lives. Most activities carried out in life have some sort of inherent risk associated with them, for example, crossing the street, eating or travelling.

Businesses can be threatened in many ways, whether it is through physical means, such as acts of nature, sabotage or terrorism, or by more subtle means, such as financial mismanagement, lack of competence or basically getting everyday project activities 'wrong'. In order to address these threats, there are several possible courses of action:

- **Elimination**: in some cases it is possible to eliminate the risk altogether. For example, if there is a risk involved with dealing with new companies for contracts with a value of over £10,000, then the simple way to eliminate this is, of course, simply not to deal with such organizations. Caution must be exercised, however, as very often one risk may be replaced by another. In the example above, there may then be a risk that it would be difficult to keep up-to-date with key technologies, as only new, dedicated companies, are exploiting them.

- **Replacement**: it is often the case that a risk may be addressed by replacing it in some way. This may be through the use of a different technology; for example, if there is a risk involved with using a specific design notation, due to possible obsolescence or limited expertise available, then replace the technique used with one that is more readily acceptable and accessible (such as the UML) which will address this problem.

- **Control**: in many cases, the risks may not be able to be eliminated nor reduced by replacement, in which case it is necessary to minimize the risk by introducing controls. These controls will vary enormously, depending on the type of risk, for example, wearing appropriate safety clothing, taking regular breaks, using only established technologies, only dealing with preferred suppliers, and so on.

- **Transfer**: transferring the risk onto a third party is considered by many as the easiest way to address risk. Although this seems like a good idea, extreme caution must be exercised, as the risk still exists and, regardless of who takes the rap, the project may fail anyway. For example, when using a financial software package for doing company accounts, there is a risk that the software will not perform the calculations correctly, in which case who takes the blame – the users or the software producers? Even in the scenario where the software producers are guaranteeing that the software will be fit for purpose, does it really help the company stay in business if the accounts system fails?

There are several key terms that must be defined so that risk management can be fully understood, managed and implemented, and these are:

- **Hazard**: anything that occurs that can lead to a risk. The terms 'hazard' and 'risk' are often confused but there are subtle differences between them; it is possible for many hazards to lead to the same risk. For example, there is a risk in a hospital that a power failure will lead to many problems, perhaps even costing the lives of some patients. There are, however, many hazards that may lead to this risk manifesting itself, such as: lightening strike, terrorist action, not paying the utility bill, lack of maintenance, and so on.

- **Risk**: defined as a product of the likelihood, or probability of the risk occurring and the effect of the hazard. In many scenarios, risk is defined either as a simple mathematical formula, *risk = probability × severity*, or in terms of a simple matrix that has one axis defining the likelihood in words and the other defining the severity of the outcome.

An important aspect of risk is the responsibility associated with it. For example, if you started smoking in the 1920s and later, as a result, developed cancer, the responsibility for the risk, it may be argued, lies with the tobacco companies. This may be argued whether or not the tobacco companies were actually aware of the risks, as everyone has a duty of care to provide safe products. The argument is that when cigarettes were sold to the general public in the 1920s, the health risks were not known and potential smokers did not think it would cause any harm. Today, however, if someone starts to smoke and develops a smoking-related illness, the responsibility is firmly on the shoulders of the smoker, as all cigarette and tobacco products now carry a government health warning that describes the risks involved in smoking.

In the UK, the Health and Safety Executive (HSE) identify five steps that are essential for any sort of risk assessment:

1. **Identification of hazards**: this can never be a complete and exhaustive list of hazards, as there are simply too many in most situations – even the most unlikely and improbable events may lead to problems. Take the smoking example: hazards will include smoking, being with smokers and being in smoky environments.

2. **Identification of who and how**: it is important to identify who or what is at risk and then to ascertain how they will be at risk. For instance, in the smoking example, the smokers will be affected directly, but what about other people who may suffer the effects of indirect passive smoking? Also, what about expectant mothers smoking and affecting their unborn children?

3. **Risk evaluation and control setting**: risk evaluation and control involves asking the question, 'how serious is the risk and is there anything that can be done to minimize it?' Consider the difference between someone walking through a smoky room, where the risk may be relatively small, compared to, say, spending three hours in a train carriage full of smokers with the windows closed. In terms of controls, consider air conditioning, opening windows, not inhaling (not recommended), and so on.

4. **Record findings**: it is important to be able to look at risks and learn from them in some way. In terms of smoking, many public places have now outlawed smoking from the premises (notice that they have not outlawed smokers, just the actual smoking activity), which is often due to customer responses, research suggesting health implications, and so on.

5. **Review**: it is important that all activities are reviewed periodically, as the hazards associated with risk often change along with the nature of the risk itself. As a final consideration of the smoking example, the hazards of smoking will shift dramatically if the government introduces a country-wide ban on smoking in enclosed public places. This means that whereas previously it was relatively safe to sit outside a pub to avoid smoke, now the situation is reversed and beer gardens will often be full of smokers. This is quite a change when one considers that beer gardens are often where children's playgrounds will be and, of course, children.

One way to reduce risk is to improve the way that things are done – or the approach. There are many approaches to solving a single problem, some of which will be higher in risk than others. If these different approaches can be captured in some way, then it is possible that they can be compared and reviewed. In fact, the way to minimize or control a risk is very often to define processes on how to avoid the risk in the first place or, when necessary, define processes concerning what to do when the risk manifests itself. Therefore, process modelling is an essential part of any risk management exercise as the solutions are often the processes that are necessary to keep everyone safe and well.

THE PROCESS

Standards, processes, procedures and guidelines

In real life, processes can manifest themselves in many different shapes or forms. When a process is written down in some way, it will often take the form of, for example, a standard, a procedure, a set of guidelines or work instructions. Although there are no absolute, globally accepted definitions for any of these terms, it is important to consider the underlying concepts and to understand them. In fact, the difference in terminology often relates to the level of detail in the process itself. Consider the following:

- Very high-level processes, such as international standards: there are many international standards bodies, such as the International Standards Organization (ISO), International Electrotechnical Commission (IEC) and European Normative (EN). Some national bodies have also obtained recognition globally and sit at the same sort of level, such as the British Standards Institution (BSI).

- High-level processes, such as industry standards: an industry standard is one that is driven by the actual industry and does not have the formal recognition of international and national standards. An industry standard may have international recognition, such as the UML or Common Object Request Broker Architecture (CORBA), or may simply be two organizations agreeing to work in the same way.

- Medium-level processes, such as in-house company standards and processes: many companies, particularly large ones, have very well-defined process models and standards and, in some cases, these may even be published, as in the case of the European Space Agency (ESA) (Mazza *et al.*, 1994).

- Low-level processes, such as in-house procedures: a typical procedure will describe how a process may be implemented. Indeed, it is possible for a single process to be implemented in different ways using different procedures.

- Very low-level processes, such as guidelines and work instructions: these will typically show a preferred or best-practice approach to carrying out a procedure. These may include specific methods and methodologies that may be applied, whether they are in-house, bespoke or commercial approaches.

The preceding list is not intended to be exhaustive, but provides a general idea of the scope of this book. The process modelling approach advocated in this book may be applied to any or all of these different types of processes.

Problems with processes

There are many problems associated with processes, which, unfortunately, often turn people off to the whole world of process modelling. In fact, mentioning processes or standards is often greeted with groans and sighs from people whose only experience has been one (or many) of disappointment. This really just goes to reinforce the fact that the whole world of process modelling is very badly affected by the three 'evils of life', described in detail in Chapter 4: complexity, lack of understanding and poor communications. So why are processes and standards so badly thought of by many people, and is this feeling justified? These two questions will be answered separately. Some of the reasons why people feel this way are discussed below:

- **Too long**: Some process descriptions are very long which, on first appearance, can be very off-putting to any potential users of the process. In fact, the length of the process description can often be misleading, as the number of pages is often not an indicator of the complexity of a process description, and it is the complexity of the process description, rather than the length of it that causes problems. However, this aside, being faced with a process description of several hundred pages is soul-destroying, regardless of how well written it may be. For example, two standards associated with process improvement are ISO 15504 (process assessment) (ISO/IEC, 2004) and CMMI (capability maturity model integrated) (Carnegie Mellon Software Engineering Institute, 2002), both of which stand at several hundred pages in length. The standard for the UML is also several hundred pages long. Although all of these standards are well written, bear in mind that, when printed out as hard copies, they each fill several volumes of folders. It is important, therefore, to be able to have a simplified representation of such a description that can be understood, at a high level, in a single glance. This will be supported by a number of other simple views, each of which can also be easily understood.

- **Too short**: Some process descriptions are very short and stand at only a few pages. Although, at first glance, such process descriptions can appear to be simple, this is often not the case. Take as an example ISO 9001 (ISO, 2000), which applies to quality systems for just about any type of organization that exists. When the standard is reduced to its actual contents (excluding front sheets, and so on) it stands at only 17 pages in length. The very fact that the standard applies to many applications means that it needs to be generic, which leads to ambiguity, an indicator of the three 'evils of life'.

- **Written by committee**: according to the old adage, you can't keep all of the people happy all of the time, which is the *raison d'être* of committees. One of the basic requirements of a committee is that it represents the viewpoints of different stakeholders. Unfortunately, this has the potential to cause as many problems as it solves and too many different viewpoints, when expressed in an unstructured way, can lead to a fragmented, ambiguous and often inconsistent process description.

- **Too many**: it is very rare indeed to find a single process model that does not relate to, or rely on some other process model. In fact, it is also rare to find a process model that relates to one or two other process models as, in real life, the number of related process models tends to be very high. Consider the situation where a process model is being created for a particular industry. For the sake of the example, let's consider a process model relating to the rail industry, but it should be borne in mind that these same principles apply to any another process model, for example, the healthcare industry. In the case of rail, the process model may have to be compatible with generic international standards, such as ISO 9001 (ISO, 2000). Also, the process model will also have to be compatible with various national and international industry-specific standards. Alongside this, consider any government or country-specific standards, safety or security standards, best practice standards and legal requirements that may have to be met. Also, we have not yet even considered any standards or procedures within the organization itself, such as Her Majesty's Railway Inspectorate (HMRI) in the UK.

- **Unrealistic**: many process descriptions have little connection to reality, which often results in a process description 'gathering dust' on a shelf through lack of use. This may be because the process is asking for too much work to be done on top of the existing working practices, such as excessive documentation, replication of existing information or requiring too much input from too many different people. If the new process differs significantly from the existing process (even if it is an informal, undocumented one), there will be a natural level of resistance to the changes. It is essential that any new process definitions are connected to existing practice wherever possible.

- **Language**: the language used by the process definition must be the one that is already used by the organization. Many companies offer 'off-the-shelf' process descriptions which, in almost all cases may be destructive unless tailored appropriately for the organization. Terminology, technical nomenclature and even marketing words and phrases must be embedded into the core process model wherever appropriate to ensure that the maximum number of people can understand the process in an unambiguous way.

- **Awareness**: for people to use a process, they must be aware of the process in the first place. This sounds like basic common sense, but the simple fact is that if a process description is printed out and left on a shelf then, in many cases, that is exactly where it will stay. With today's technology and the ubiquitous nature of the internet and web browsers, it is a relatively simple matter to make process descriptions available to people via their desktops. Of courses, this will only work in places where people sit at computers but, even if people do not have computer access, the fact remains that the process descriptions must be readily available to the people who are supposed to using them. The process descriptions should also make people's lives easier, rather than being an overhead (in terms of time). It is not until people can see the benefit of having this information to hand that they will truly start to adopt the whole process ethos effectively.

- **Fear of failure**: a common complaint when it comes to any sort of process modelling and process description is that the whole exercise is a waste of time because 'we tried it three years ago and it didn't work'. Just because something has been attempted once and failed, does not mean that it will never work. The actual underlying cause of these failures needs to be investigated. In almost every case where this has happened, it is relatively simple to see that all the information required for the process description was not present or that the problems discussed in this section have occurred. One of the main aims of this book is to introduce and define a process meta-model that can be used as a checklist for ensuring a complete and effective process description. By using this meta-model as a basis for an investigation, it is very common to see exactly why the previous process exercise has failed – one or more of the views required by the process meta-model is missing or incomplete.

- **Perception**: the perception of the process is key. People must be aware of the value of effective processes. A lack of understanding here may be due to poor education in the application, use and consequent benefits of the process.

These are just some of the common reasons why the process modelling exercise fails. This book intends to minimize the potential time and effort that is wasted by many organizations in pursuit of their process modelling requirements. Remember, process modelling is not magic, but nor is it a mundane task. There is a deep level of understanding required in order to produce an effective process model and description.

Modelling techniques

There are many modelling techniques that have been used extensively, and with varying degrees of success, for many years. Many of these techniques are based on visual techniques or, to put it another way, drawing diagrams to represent processes. The list of these techniques includes, but is not limited to:

- **Flow charts**: the classic graphical modelling language that most people have come across at some point in their lives, even if it has nothing to do with software. Although widely used, flow charts are frequently misused and are poorly understood. The biggest problem with flow charts, however, is that they only realize a single view of the process model and, as discussed later in this book, there are seven views required for effective and complete process modelling.

- **RACI matrix tables**: RACI stands for 'responsible', 'accountable', 'consulted' and 'informed' and RACI matrix tables are used to relate process activity to stakeholder roles. According to the RACI approach, any activity within a process will have a number of stakeholder roles associated with it, and these roles may be responsible (they do the work for the activity), accountable (they are responsible for the success or failure of the activity), consulted (they are asked to participate in the activity) or informed (they have information concerning the activity distributed to them). Basic RACI matrix tables are just that – a simple table for cross-referencing between the roles and the activity. However, these tables are often used in conjunction with flow charts but are often contorted to include some sort of behaviour which makes the tables more complex and adds little value.

- **BPML**: the Business Process Modelling Language. The BPML is the result of the business process modelling initiative (BPMI), whose aim is to provide a notation that can be readily understood by all business users and that ensures that various business execution languages can be visualized (BPMI, 2002). The three main aims are to define the notation and its association semantics and to amalgamate all best practice modelling notations (interestingly enough, including the UML). Although this is an excellent initiative that has yielded very good results, the BPML is far too narrow to meet the stringent requirements for process modelling identified in this book. The notation itself focuses entirely on the behavioural aspect of the process model which, although adequate for the scope identified in the BPMI, is not considered wide enough for the purposes of this book. Indeed, the introduction of the process meta-model will show that there are seven views that need to be considered – four of which are realized by structural diagrams, for which the BPML has no facility. Also, the BPML does not consider the requirements for a process that are essential for any sort of process validation. This means that, in total, the BPML could only be used to realize two of the seven views required for effective and complete process modelling.

This is just a small sample of some of the techniques that are available for use. Although the technique adopted in this book is the UML, the main focus of the book is a series of concepts that can be realized using any modelling notation that is capable of meeting the modelling requirements of the process.

The UML

This book uses diagrams to help to visualize and understand processes at many different levels. These diagrams are not random and are actually part of a larger 'language'. The language chosen is the UML, which is a *visual modelling language*:

- **visual**: the results can be seen graphically or, to put it another way, it is a language of diagrams containing symbols;
- **modelling**: reality is simplified in some way so that it can be more easily understood;
- **language**: it is a means of communication.

The choice of the language itself has a certain rationale. The UML is the most widely used modelling language in the world today. Although the UML has its roots firmly in the software world, it is increasingly being used for wider, more systems-based applications.

There are also several pragmatic reasons for choosing the UML:

- **Widespread use**: the UML is the most widely used modelling language in the world. Up until relatively recently, there were more than 100 visual modelling techniques and notations available to software engineers. However, the UML has now superseded all of them – with the full assent of every methodologist in the world. Although the UML originated in the software world, the notation itself can be applied to almost any form of modelling.

- **Accepted internationally**: the UML is not just limited to a particular country or continent, but is a truly world-wide standard that is accepted just about everywhere. This means that when working with colleagues in different countries, there is a common medium on which to base discussions.

- **ISO standard**: the UML is now an ISO standard – ISO 19501 (2005), which gives it more credibility than it just being an industry standard. Many of the criticisms that were aimed at the UML were concerns about its lack of international credibility, which are now resolved.

- **UK government mandate, via eGIF**: as the UML becomes more widely accepted, it also becomes more formally accepted by world organizations, such as governments. One example of this is in the UK, where there is an initiative named *eGIF: The electronic government interoperability framework* (Cabinet Office, 2004). The main aim behind the eGIF is to define the technical policies and specifications governing information flows across government and the public sector. It covers interconnectivity, data integration, e-services access and content management. This initiative will apply not only to organizations who deal directly with government bodies, but also many of their subcontractors.

- **Intuitive**: the notation used by the UML is, when used properly, simple and intuitive. Some aspects of the UML are more intuitive than others, which is due in part to some elements of the UML looking like previous techniques, such as flow charts and data flow diagrams. This familiarity increases the perception that something is easier to understand.

- **Extensive use in other aspects of the organization**: this final advantage of using the UML is often overlooked but can have a massive impact on issues such as training. Consider an organization where there are managers, engineers, technicians, quality assurers, marketers, directors and sales teams. If each of these has a very basic idea of the core elements of the language and is familiar with one or two of the diagrams, then there is a massive increase in communication effectiveness. Of course, different people in different jobs will naturally use different techniques and tools to perform their work, but if the core *knowledge* behind the work is defined in a common language, then this knowledge can be turned into effective value in the business. For example, using a single core notation in training will decrease the number of different techniques being used, hence enabling a single, common view to be communicated by and to all members of staff by an effective training unit or partner. Also, in the case of process modelling, if the core company knowledge is captured in a process model, then there is a ready-made training course for anyone who understand the basics of the UML language. After all, what better source for training material than the actual knowledge itself!

Therefore, the notation used in this book is the UML. You do not have to be an expert in UML to appreciate how it is used, nor to start using it – the expertise will come with time. Also, the use of UML in this book is limited to a very small subset of the actual language, which minimizes the learning curve. Providing that the core concepts of the rationale for modelling is understood, the use of the notation is relatively straightforward.

CONCLUSIONS

This chapter introduced and explained the background of process modelling. It briefly explored the concept of risk and introduced the application of process modelling to control risk. Central to this, the chapter discussed the idea of processes and why they are so important, together with some problems that are often associated with processes. In fact, processes are far more complex than meets the eye; hence, the need for process modelling. If processes are going to be modelled, an appropriate language is required and, from the various languages and notations available, the Unified Modelling Language, or UML, was identified as the most appropriate.

The remainder of this book builds on these foundations to create an entire approach to pragmatic business process modelling that is based on best modelling practice and uses an internationally recognized standard notation for its realization.

2 The UML Diagrams

'Oo-bi-doo! I wanna be like you-oo-oo. I wanna walk like you, talk like you do!'
King Louis, *The Jungle Book*, Walt Disney

INTRODUCTION

In order to understand the magic behind processes it is first necessary to have an effective analysis and communication tool available for the task. In this book, the tool used is the UML.

This chapter introduces the diagrams that will be used as part of the process modelling approach described in this book, all of which are part of the UML. The information in this chapter presents only a small subset of the UML and focuses on only the parts of the language that are relevant for process modelling.

MODELLING

The UML can be an intimidating language at first appearances, particularly to people who do not necessarily have a background in technology or modelling. However, like any other language, all parts of the language are rarely used at the same time and certain subsets of the UML lend themselves to particular applications. In this instance, we shall be looking at the small subset of the UML that applies to process modelling.

Before looking at the diagrams that will be used, it is first necessary to look at some basic concepts involved with modelling and, in particular, the UML.

When modelling any sort of system, it is important to understand a few requirements with which any decent modelling language should be able to cope. These are generic requirements for any form of modelling and are not specific to the UML.

Before looking at the four basic requirements for any sort of modelling, it is worth revisiting the reasoning behind modelling.

- A model is a simplification of reality.
- We model in order to:
  - increase our understanding;
  - identify areas of complexity; and
  - ease communication.

- We have to do this because, as human beings, we cannot comprehend complexity.

Bearing in mind the driving force behind modelling, it is important to have some sort of common language that can be used as a modelling medium. In order to choose an effective modelling language, it is first necessary to understand the four basic requirements of modelling any system, described below:

- **The choice of model**: there are many correct ways to represent any sort of system, but it is important to choose the most appropriate way. Almost everyone will remember back in their schooldays when teachers used to say (and still do) that you get the marks for the working out or, to put it another way, for showing your choice of approach. To put this into a process modelling context, a process is simply an approach to doing something, therefore choosing an appropriate process is crucial for getting something right, for running a successful project and for demonstrating quality. Choosing an inappropriate approach, or process model, can be very costly.

- **The abstraction of the model**: it is essential to look at any system at different levels of abstraction, or detail. For example, imagine looking at the plans for a house, where there would be an overall, high-level view of the house, maybe showing just the exterior and the surrounding area. Also, supporting this, there will be plans for each storey of the house, each room on each floor, the interconnections between floors and so on. In fact, some aspects of the plan will be very low-level or finely detailed aspects of the house, such as an individual window fixing that may have a drawing all to itself.

- **The connection to reality**: a model is a simplification of reality and, because of this, there is an inherent danger with modelling – it is possible (and, in some cases, easy) to miss off either too much information or relevant information from a model.

- **Different views**: consider for one last time, the example of the house. Consider the different people that will be involved in its construction, such as builders, carpenters and electricians. Each of these different people will require different pieces of information – the electrician will only be interested in the wiring diagram and where the wires will run in the house, whereas the carpenter will be less concerned about the electricity but, rather, be more concerned with the doors, windows, and so on. Different people have different views and, hence, require different sorts of information. Paramount to this, however, is that all information must be consistent as each different piece of information is merely a different view on a common model and it is important to get the model correct by matching up the views.

It is now time to look at the language that has been chosen to carry out the modelling – the UML.

THE UML

The aim of modelling is to create a model that will help to identify and manage complexity, aid understanding and to improve communications. The UML provides a toolkit of 13 diagrams. Each diagram may be used to realize a number of views on the model. Each diagram represents a slightly different view of the model and is analogous to opening a small window onto the model. Enough of these windows must be opened to provide a full specification of the model and to provide enough confidence that the model is correct. In most cases, it is not necessary to use all the diagrams; rather, a small subset of diagrams is used. In the case of process modelling, we shall be looking at a subset of four diagrams: the class diagram, the activity diagram, the sequence diagram and the use case diagram.

Modelling using the UML

Real life is inherently complex and, therefore, in order to understand and be able to communicate any information concerning real life, it is important to model this information. As discussed previously, this modelling may take the form of mathematical equations, pictures, formal diagrams, text descriptions, and so on. However, even these simplified representations of reality – the models – are themselves very complex. In order to model effectively, it is important to have some sort of structure to the modelling notation adopted, which is where the UML comes in. The UML is used to visualize a model by drawing a number of diagrams to represent different views of the model.

Any model has two distinct aspects in the UML, the structural aspect and the behavioural aspect:

- The structural aspect of the model shows the 'what' of the model – what entities exist, what relationships exist between them, what each entity looks like and what each entity does.
- The behavioural aspect of the model shows the 'how' of the model – in what order things happen, under what conditions, timing concepts, sequencing and scenarios.

Each of these two aspects of the model *must* exist in order for the model to be fully specified and these two aspects *must* be consistent with one another. In order to visualize these two aspects of the model, a number of UML diagrams exist that are used to represent either structural or behavioural aspects of the model. Each of these diagrams will represent some sort of *view* of the model, and all these views will combine to form a complete specification of the model. Despite the fact the model is a simplification of the very complex reality, it must be borne in mind that

19

this model, when considered in its entirely, still has the potential to be complex. Think of the model as a large, complex beast, consisting of ever-changing and shifting swirling lines, that is quite incomprehensible. Each time a diagram is created, it is like opening a window into a very small part of the complex model. Each time one of these windows is opened, a very simple representation of the view out of the window is constructed.

The UML language

The UML is a language that aids the understanding of a model by representing it graphically. Any UML model will be made up of a number of views of the system and each of these views will be realized using one or more of the diagrams that make up the UML language. In the UML, there are 13 different types of diagram, although, for the purposes of this book, we will only be looking at a subset of four diagrams: the class diagram, the activity diagram, the sequence diagram and the use case diagram.

The remainder of this chapter is intended to be used as a reference for future modelling and, although only four of the 13 UML diagrams are covered, there is still a lot of information for readers who are completely new to the field of modelling to take in. It is recommended, therefore, that if you have little or no modelling experience you should read this chapter in separate sittings, rather than trying to understand it all on one occasion.

Each diagram has the same basic structure, as they are made up of 'nodes' (usually shapes of some description) that are joined together via 'paths' (usually represented by lines of some description). Each diagram is described in terms of its modelling elements and then an example of the use of that diagram is introduced and discussed. You may find it easier to look at the graphical notation and the example at the same time, to enforce the connection between the modelling elements and how they appear on a diagram.

THE CLASS DIAGRAM

Class diagrams represent a structural aspect of the system and have many uses. They allow conceptual 'things' to be drawn and the relationships between these identified. Class diagrams form the backbone of any UML model and will have consistency relationships with all the other diagrams used for process modelling.

Class diagram concepts and notation

The graphical notation for the elements that make up a class diagram are shown in Figure 2.1.

The basic elements of a class diagram are the *class* and the *relationship*.

- A *class* represents a conceptual thing and is usually a noun. A good way to understand the nature of a class is to think of it as a template

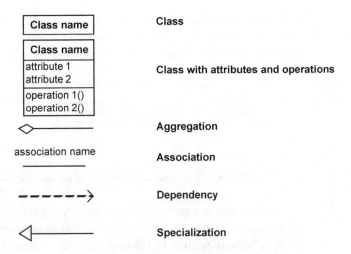

FIGURE 2.1 *Graphical notation for class diagrams*

for something. For example, the class Person would represent all people generally, rather than a specific person. A specific person is known as an *instance*. Classes are represented graphically by rectangles and can be further described by identifying *attributes* and *operations*. Classes form the basic nodes in the class diagram.

- A *relationship* represents the identification of a conceptual relationship between one or more classes. A relationship is represented graphically by variations on a line, depending on the type of relationship. There are four types of relationship that are used for process modelling: the *association*, the *aggregation*, the *generalization/ specialization* and the *dependency*. Relationships form the basic paths in the class diagram.

The class diagram can be defined in more detail, but these are the two basic elements at its core.

Representing classes

The graphical notation of a class is shown in Figure 2.2, in which there are two classes, each represented as a rectangle. This is a valid UML diagram, but one would have to question the value of a diagram where only two disparate classes are shown, although, as will be seen later in this book, the lack of information on a diagram can often be as revealing as the amount of information present.

FIGURE 2.2 *Graphical notation of a class*

In order to relate two or more classes together, a relationship is used. The most basic type of relationship is known as an association and identifies a simple conceptual relationship between one or more classes.

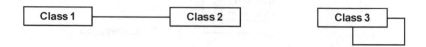

FIGURE 2.3 *Graphical notation of an association relationship*

The diagram in Figure 2.3 shows two examples of the graphical notation for an association relationship. On the left-hand side of the diagram, there is an association that is relating together 'Class 1' and 'Class 2'. This diagram would be read as 'Class 1 is associated with Class 2'. It is also possible to have an association related back to the same class, as shown on the right-hand side of the diagram. In this case, the diagram, would be read as 'Class 3 is associated with Class 3' or, 'Class 3 is associated with itself'.

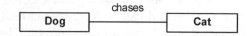

FIGURE 2.4 *Naming an association*

The association itself should always be described by a piece of text, as shown in Figure 2.4, to make the diagram easier to understand. This diagram should be read as 'Dog chases Cat' and this sentence, when read out loud, should make sense to a third party. However, as is the case in this diagram, an incomplete diagram can be open to misunderstanding. For example, there is nothing on the diagram to indicate which way the diagram should be read – left-to-right, or right-to-left. Although many people would automatically read left-to-right, in a diagram of any reasonable size or complexity, it is impossible to organize all the elements of a diagram in a left-to-right fashion. Also, by reading from left-to-right, people are often assuming a logical order of things occurring or happening, and this is not the information that is conveyed on a class diagram.

Figure 2.5 indicates the direction of the association with a small triangle, showing that the direction is left-to-right. Therefore, this diagram

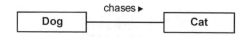

FIGURE 2.5 *Showing direction on an association*

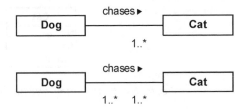

FIGURE 2.6 *Showing numbers on classes*

definitely says 'Dog chases Cat' and cannot be read the other way around. However, there is room for ambiguity even on a diagram that is this simple. Consider the question 'how many cats and how many dogs?' At the moment, there is no indication of the ratio of cats to dogs, so this needs to be cleared up before the diagram can be read correctly.

Figure 2.6 shows the association between 'Dog' and 'Cat', but this time there are two variations shown that differ because of the numbers (or 'multiplicity') involved. Numbers are indicated on the ends of associations and use a simple, intuitive system.

- Numbers are represented as simple numerical characters, therefore, to indicate the number five, the digit '5' would be shown. The only exception to this is the situation where the number is one, and this can be indicated by either showing the digit '1' or by leaving the end of the association empty. Any association without a number indicated is assumed to be '1'.

- A range of numbers is represented as the extremities of the range with dots between. Therefore, to indicate a range between two and five, the association would have a multiplicity of '2..5'. A star can also indicate that a range is open-ended, which is useful, because it is very common. For example, to indicate one or more, the association would have a multiplicity of '1..*'.

- A series of numbers is represented by simple set of digits. Therefore, one, two or three is indicated as '1, 2, 3', six, nine, 11 or 20 is represented by '6, 9, 11, 20', and so on. The only exception to this is where there are two consecutive numbers in a sequence where the series or range syntax can be used. Therefore, to indicate zero or one, the multiplicity could be either '0..1' or '0,1'.

The upper half of the diagram, therefore, is read as 'Dog chases one or more Cat'. Note that no number is indicated on the 'Dog' side of the association, therefore the number is assumed to be '1'. It is important to understand that the numbers indicate a *ratio* rather than absolute numbers, so a more correct way to read the diagram would be 'each Dog chases one or more Cat'. The inclusion of the word 'each' here

FIGURE 2.7 *Examples of attributes for the class 'Cat'*

conveys the fact that there may be many dogs, each of which will chase a number of cats, rather than saying that there is only a single dog. This could represent anything from one dog chasing one cat, right up to a dog chasing a herd of cats.

The lower half of the diagram, although looking very similar, has a subtly different meaning and should be read as 'one or more Dog chases one or more Cat'. This could represent anything from a dog chasing a single cat, to a pack of dogs chasing a single cat, to a pack of dogs chasing a herd of cats, and anything in-between.

Classes can also be defined in more detail by identifying their features and their behaviour or, to put it another way, what each class looks like and what it does.

The features of a class are known as 'attributes' and are usually nouns that can have different values associated with them.

Figure 2.7 shows the class of 'Cat' with its features identified as attributes. In this example, three attributes have been identified: 'Name', 'Age' and 'Colour'. It is important that attribute names are chosen effectively and one way to ensure this is to think about the different sorts of values that an attribute may take, for example:

- 'Name' could be a text string.

- 'Age' could be a integer or a real number, depending on the requirements of the model. It may also be desirable to indicate a range here, so that 'Age' could be defined as an integer somewhere between zero and 20. This would be shown as 'Age:int(0..20)'.

- 'Colour' could be a text string, or a list of predefined colours, or a number to indicate the colour, a hexadecimal representation of the colour, and so on.

In fact, just by thinking about the sort of values that an attribute can take can really help in understanding the model. Consider, for example, if an attribute was identified as 'Black', would this be correct? In many cases, the answer would be 'no' as the attribute cannot take on different values – in fact it may very well be that the author of the model intended to represent 'Colour' but, instead, used the term 'Black'. However, there is also an argument that 'Black' is a correct attribute if the intention was only to find out whether the cat is black or not. In such a case, the attribute value would be Boolean. It may be that the model is intended to be used for customers who are all witches, in which case they are only interested in

FIGURE 2.8 *Example of operations for the class 'Cat'*

whether the cat is black or not (witches, as any child can confirm, always have black cats!).

It is also possible to identify the behaviour of a class by identifying *operations*. An operation is usually a verb and represents something that the class does.

Figure 2.8 shows the operations that have been identified for the class 'Cat'. The operations represent what the behaviour is – *not how the class behaves*. Remember that the class diagram is a structural diagram and, as such, shows the 'what' of a system, not the 'how'. The operations are as follows:

- 'eat', which could be further described by stating what type of food is eaten, the amount, and so on, and which information can be shown in the brackets after the operation name; in this example, the operation may be further specified as 'eat(food_type, amount, frequency)';
- 'sleep', which may be further described by stating the length of the sleep, the location, and so on, for example 'sleep(duration, location)';
- 'run', which may be further described by stating the speed, direction, and so on, for example 'run(speed, direction)'.

Of course, it is entirely possible to leave the brackets empty and, in reality, this is often the case with process modelling, but the mechanism for further specification is there if required.

Representing relationships

In the same way that classes can be described in more detail by adding attributes and operations, it is also possible to define relationships in more detail by considering different types of relationship. These basic different types of relationship are defined as part of the standard UML language. The four basic relationship types that will be used are: associations, aggregations, specializations and dependencies.

Association

An association is the most basic type of relationship and is used for expressing simple conceptual relationships between two classes. The association relationship has been used several times already in this chapter

25

and can be seen in Figures 2.3, 2.4, 2.5 and 2.6. An association allows classes to be related together and should be very easily read and understood by anyone looking at the diagram.

Aggregation

An aggregation allows an 'is made up of' relationship between classes and allows the structure of a class to be broken down into a number of component classes. This is a very powerful mechanism that allows hierarchies and structures to be expressed, at several levels, on a single diagram.

Figure 2.9 shows a number of aggregation relationships that depict the hierarchy of the structure of the main class 'Process model'. The diagram shows that the main class 'Process model' is made up of one or more 'Process group', each of which is made up of one or more 'Process'. Note how numbers are indicated in exactly the same way as with a standard association. At the bottom of the diagram there are three aggregation relationships, all from the class 'Process' to the classes 'Role', 'Artefact' and 'Activity'. Although there are three aggregations on this diagram, it is usual to overlap them, as has been done on Figure 2.10, to facilitate reading the diagrams.

Figure 2.10 has exactly the same meaning as Figure 2.9, the only difference being that the three aggregations in that diagram have been overlaid so that they appear as a single aggregation with three branches.

Specialization

The specialization relationship allows a 'has types' relationship to be defined, which can be used to classify classes into different 'types of' groups. This is a natural way to express information, particularly when different elements of a similar nature need to be differentiated in some way. This relationship is indicated graphically by a triangle symbol which should be read as either 'has types' if reading the diagram downwards, or as 'is a type of' when reading upwards.

Figure 2.11 shows four specializations from the class 'Process group'. This diagram is read as: 'Process group has types of: Enterprise, Project, Agreement and Technical' if reading from top-to-bottom. If the diagram was being read from bottom-to-top, then it would be read as 'Enterprise, Project, Agreement and Technical are all types of Process group'.

It is possible to have many levels of nesting in the specialization hierarchy that make use of a feature known as *inheritance*. Inheritance specifies that any features of a parent class are inherited by all its child classes. A parent class is a class that has subtypes defined below it, whereas a child class is a class that is a subtype of a parent class. It is possible for a class to be both a parent of one class and a child of a different class, as shown in Figure 2.12.

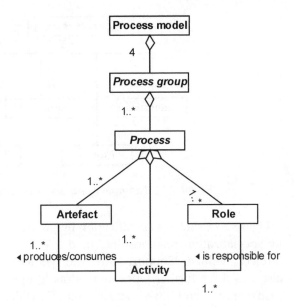

FIGURE 2.9 *Example of the aggregation relationship*

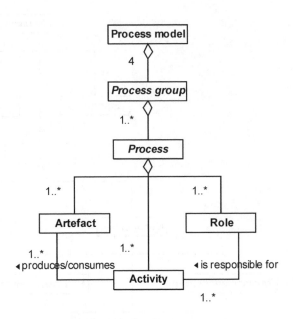

FIGURE 2.10 *Overlapping aggregations to tidy up a diagram*

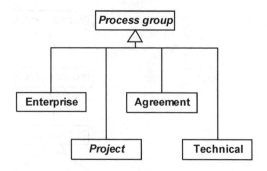

FIGURE 2.11 *Example of the specialization relationship*

Figure 2.12 shows a classification hierarchy with many levels, all related by specialization relationships. In this example, there are two types of 'Project' defined: 'Support' and 'Management'. The class 'Management' also has three further types defined as 'Project management', 'Resource management' and 'Risk management'. Consider, as an example, the class 'Resource management'. This class is a type of 'Management', which is a type of 'Project', which is a type of 'Process group'. Therefore, it follows that 'Resource management' is actually a type of 'Process group', albeit via several levels of nesting. 'Process group' has an attribute of 'Identifier' defined and this attribute is inherited by all its child classes. Therefore, the

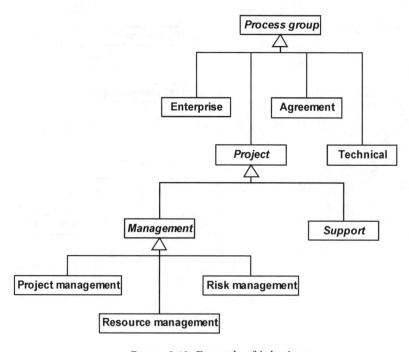

FIGURE 2.12 *Example of inheritance*

classes 'Enterprise', 'Project', 'Agreement' and Technical' all inherit the attribute directly from 'Process group'. The classes 'Support' and 'Management' also inherit the same attribute from 'Process group', this time indirectly via the class 'Project'. Finally, the three classes 'Project management', Risk management' and 'Resource management' all inherit the same attribute.

Inheritance also works for operations and any structures that are defined for a parent class, such as an aggregation. This is something that will be explored later in this book.

Notice how several of the classes have their names italicized, such as '*Project*' and '*Management*'. This indicates that the class is 'abstract' in that it has no instances. This is usually used when a class is showing a classification or grouping and has no real-life instances.

The term 'specialization' is often used with the term 'generalization' – either with the two terms used at the same time (specialization/generalization) or one term being used in preference to the other. This is because the specialization relationship can be read either top-down or bottom-up and each term reflects this. If the diagram is read from top to bottom, the classes get more specialized the further down the hierarchy that they occur. Likewise, if the diagram is read from the bottom to the top, then the classes get more generalized the further up the hierarchy they occur.

Dependency

The final type of relationship is the dependency. A dependency is used to relate two classes in a tightly coupled way, which implies that as one class changes, so will its dependent classes. There are many uses for this, one of the main uses being to express instances of classes.

A dependency is shown graphically by a dashed directed line between two classes. The class with the arrow next to it is the dependent class and, conversely, the one without an arrow is the governing class (see Figure 2.13).

Figure 2.13 shows three dependencies that are related to the 'Stakeholder requirements' class. The dependency relationship is used in different ways here:

- **To represent instances of a class**: the two elements 'Project X :Stakeholder requirements' and 'Project Y :Stakeholder requirements' represent instances, or real-life examples, of the class 'Stakeholder'. In order to differentiate between one of these instances (also known as objects) and a normal class, the text in the instance box is underlined and a colon precedes the name of the class. It is also possible to provide an identifier for each instance; in this case the identifiers 'Project X' and 'Project Y' have been used. Remembering that classes are abstract and define templates for real-life things, the instances represent these real-life things. Therefore, in the example shown in

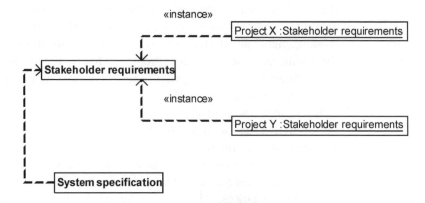

FIGURE 2.13 *Example of dependencies*

Figure 2.13, the class represents the template for the process known as 'Stakeholder requirements', whereas the two instances represent real-life examples or executions of this process. This instance relationship is also shown here with the dependency relationship (the dotted line) by the word 'instance' with chevrons around it. In summary, therefore, the <<instance>> dependency relates instances and classes – the real to the abstract.

- **Normal dependency**: the second type of dependency used in Figure 2.13 is just a simple dependency that implies that the two classes have a very strong relationship. In this case, the class 'System specification' is dependent upon the class 'Stakeholder requirements', as they share some of the same content, which is generated by the 'Stakeholder requirements' class. Therefore, when the 'Stakeholder requirements' class changes, so does the 'System specification' class – hence the dependency relationship. In summary, therefore, the normal use of dependencies relates two classes – abstract to abstract.

Dependencies should be used sparingly in class diagrams as it is easy to misuse them when a normal association would be more appropriate.

Using class diagrams for process modelling

Class diagrams are used to realize four of the views from the process meta-model, which are:

- **the process structure view**, where classes are used to define the basic terminology and process structure for the whole process model;
- **the process content view**, where classes are used to represent actual processes, with their relevant artefacts and activities represented as attributes and operations respectively;

- **the stakeholder view**, where classes are used to represent the stakeholder roles in the system, along with relationships between them;

- **the information view**, where classes are used to represent the artefacts in the system and the relationships between them.

Each of these diagrams will be explained in more detail in Chapter 4.

THE ACTIVITY DIAGRAM

The activity diagram realizes a behavioural aspect of the overall model and is used to model low-level, or detailed, behaviour. The activity diagram has strong relationships with the class diagram. Activity diagrams look familiar to many people, as they are derived from flowcharts. Most people will have seen a variant of a flowchart at some point in their lives, hence many people find the activity diagram a friendly diagram to work with.

The activity diagram shows the 'how', or the behaviour, of a single class. A class diagram identifies attributes and operations, but doesn't specify in which order operations are executed, nor the information flow. The activity diagram does both of these and more. One key feature of an activity diagram, essential for process modelling, is that it enables the definition of responsibility for activities within a process.

Activity diagram concepts and notation

The basic graphical notation for the activity diagram is shown in Figure 2.14.

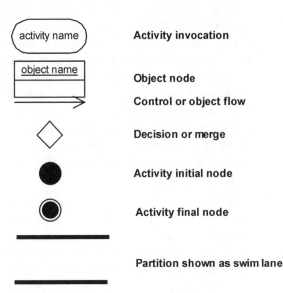

FIGURE 2.14 *Graphical notation for activity diagrams*

The basic elements within the activity diagram are:

- **The activity invocation**: an activity invocation is the execution of an operation taken from its owner-class (the class whose behaviour is being defined by the activity diagram). An activity invocation must exist for each operation from the owner-class, and vice versa. An activity invocation is represented graphically by a rectangle with two straight sides (top and bottom) and two completely rounded sides (left and right); in other words, a sausage shape. Each activity invocation represents the processes of some sort of information and it is also possible to represent activity invocations that receive, or send, messages from, and to, the outside world. These are known as *signals*. These signals are represented graphically by irregular pentagons with one end being either convex (to represent an outgoing signal) or concave (to represent an incoming signal). The activity invocations form the basic nodes in the activity diagram.

- **Control and object flows**: activity invocations must be executed in a particular order, and the control and object flows define this order, by relating activity invocations together in an ordered flow. Both control and object flows are represented graphically by directed lines, the ends of which attach to activity invocations. The control and object flows form the basic paths in the class diagram.

- **Control fork and joins**: the flow of control, represented by the control and object flows, can be split up in concurrent flows using control forks and joins. A control fork splits a single flow into any number of concurrent flows that may, or may not be executed in parallel. These split flows can then be joined back together using the control join. The activity diagram uses the concept of 'token flow', which means that, for each flow, there is a conceptual token that can be used to track its current progress. In order for a set of flows to be joined together, each must present its token to the control join before the overall flow can progress. Another way to think about this is to imagine that all concurrent control flows must complete before they can be rejoined. Both control forks and joins are represented graphically by thick black lines with a single flow entering and multiple flows leaving (in the case of the fork), or multiple flows entering and a single flow exiting (in the case of a control join). Control forks and joins form nodes in the activity diagram.

- **Object nodes**: objects are used to represent information flow within the activity diagram, which is useful for showing the inputs and outputs of each activity invocation. They can be represented as instances on the diagram (a rectangle with the class name underlined and a preceding colon) or by simply showing text on a line. The choice between which to use is usually dependent on which makes the diagram more readable. For example, text is easier to use for showing

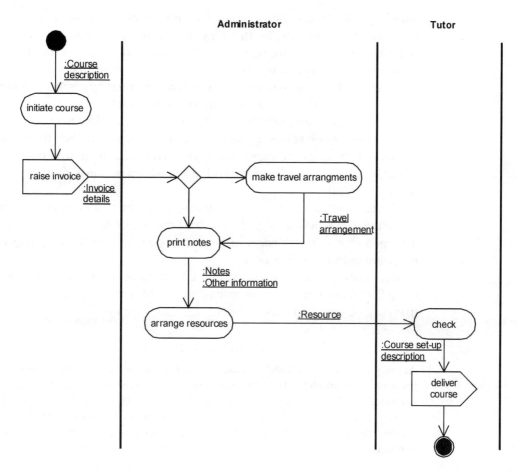

FIGURE 2.15 *Example of an activity diagram*

simple information flow between two activity invocations. If, on the other hand, the information flow is coming in from somewhere else in the system, it is more usual to show the full graphical syntax of the rectangle.

- **Start and end states**: each activity diagram must start and end. This represents the creation and destruction respectively of an instance of the owner-class. A start state is represented graphically by a filled-in circle, whereas an end state is represented by a bulls-eye symbol.

- **Swim lanes**: swim lanes represent regions on an activity diagram and are used for allocating responsibility to activity invocations. A swim lane is represented graphically by two parallel lines that partition the diagram and encapsulate a number of activity invocations. Note that responsibility is allocated to the activity invocations, rather than the objects that flow in and out of them.

Figure 2.15 shows an example of an activity diagram. The diagram is divided into a number of swim lanes that are represented by the vertical lines that divide up the diagram and that each have the name of a stakeholder at the top. In this way, any activity invocations that are contained within a life line are under the responsibility of the stakeholder at the top of the swim lane. Each activity invocation represents a calling of an operation from the parent class and is represented by a sausage shape on the diagram. Inputs and outputs to each activity invocation can be shown by objects, that may be represented graphically by boxes or, in the case of complex diagrams, by simple text associated with each transition.

The activity diagram shows the logical control and information flow through an instance of a class and also assigns responsibility for each activity invocation.

It is also possible to show where messages are transmitted or received by the activity diagram as signals – a transmit signal is represented by a pentagon with a convex edge, whereas a receive signal is represented by a pentagon with a concave edge.

Other concepts, such as concurrent execution of control, can be shown using flow forks and joins, where the flow is split between different threads that may be executed concurrently.

Using activity diagrams for process modelling

Activity diagrams are used to realize the 'process behaviour view' from the process meta-model. The process behaviour view is a set of activity diagrams, each of which describes the behaviour of a single process. The activity diagram is used exclusively for the 'process behaviour view' in the process meta-model, and is related directly to classes from the 'process content view'.

THE SEQUENCE DIAGRAM

Introduction

The sequence diagram realizes a behavioural aspect of the overall model and is used to model high-level behaviour. The sequence diagram is an excellent diagram for tying different views of the system together and forms the basis of the process validation of the process meta-model.

Sequence diagram concepts and notation

The graphical notation for a sequence diagram is shown in Figure 2.16.
The basic elements within a sequence diagram are:

- **Interactions**: an interaction is a representation of an ordered set of activities that are executed in order to fulfil a particular requirement or, to put it another way, an interaction is a scenario. Each interaction is defined using a sequence diagram and each sequence diagram has a frame around it that identifies the particular interaction. Any one of these interactions can now be called up during any other interaction

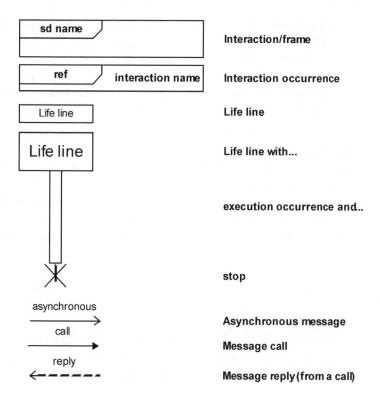

	Interaction/frame
	Interaction occurrence
	Life line
	Life line with...
	execution occurrence and..
	stop
	Asynchronous message
	Message call
	Message reply (from a call)

FIGURE 2.16 *Graphical notation for sequence diagrams*

so that interactions may be nested. When an interaction is called up during another interaction, it is called an 'interaction occurrence'. The graphical notation for an interaction is a large box that contains the sequence diagram, with a small pentagon in the top left-hand corner containing its name. An interaction occurrence has the same graphical symbol except, this time, there is no sequence diagram within it. Therefore, the symbol is far smaller. Instead of the name of the interaction in the label box, the term 'ref' is used to indicate that this interaction is defined elsewhere, and the name of the interaction is written in the main body of the symbol, where the sequence diagram is usually located. Interactions may be represented by an entire sequence diagram or, indeed, may be called up as single interaction occurrences that are defined on other diagrams.

- **Life lines**: a life line represents an instance, or collection of instances, of a class. A life line is represented graphically by a box with the name of the parent class in it, with a dashed vertical line underneath it. This line represents time, going down the page. A life line represents a graphical node on the diagram.

35

- **Messages**: a message is the basic communication mechanism between life lines and can represent almost any form of information exchange. This could be a true data exchange or may be a simple control message exchange. These messages may be as simple or complex as required but, in the examples shown here, will be kept deliberately at quite a high level.

Figure 2.17 depicts a simple sequence diagram. The boxes across the top of the diagram represent the instances of classes, or life lines, as they are known. Each lifeline has a dashed line going down the page underneath it, that represents time going down the page – the top of the line representing the earliest time and the bottom of the line representing the latest time. Interactions between life lines are represented by messages that are passed between the dashed lines, and are described by a text identifier on top of the line. This identifier may also include any important information that is required by the message, shown in brackets after the identifier name. It is also possible to show conditions that may have to be met before a message can be sent or received by showing the logical condition in square brackets.

In this way, it is possible to describe the sequence of events (going down the page), the messages passed between the life lines, and any logical condition or any information that is passed between the life lines.

Using sequence diagrams for process modelling

Sequence diagram are used in the process meta-model to realize the process instance views. These process instance views are used to represent *scenarios* associated with particular requirements that are used to validate requirements. This is discussed in more detail in Chapter 4.

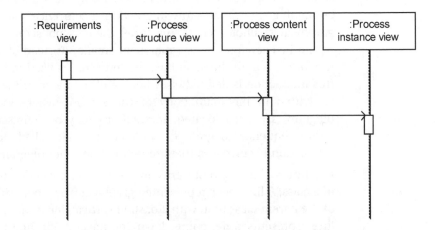

FIGURE 2.17 *Example of a sequence diagram*

THE USE CASE DIAGRAM

The use case diagram realizes a behavioural aspect of the overall model and is used to model the behaviour of the system at its highest, or context, level. The use case diagram is used exclusively for modelling requirements and context in the UML and, although very simple to look at, it is perhaps the most difficult diagram to get right.

Use case diagram concepts and notation

The basic notation for the use case diagram is shown in Figure 2.18.
The use case diagram has the following main elements:

- **Actors:** an actor represents a stakeholder role and is represented graphically by a 'stick person'. The stick person symbol is particularly confusing as, not unreasonably, many people assume that it represents a person, but this is not the case. The stick person, or actor, represents the *role* taken by a person, thing, organization or place and, as such, is not actually a person in real life. Caution must be exercised when identifying and defining actors in a use case diagram. All actors sit *outside* the boundary of the system that is being modelled and interact in some way with the system, in that each actor will have some relationship with an aspect of functionality of the system, which is represented by 'use cases'. Actors represent graphical nodes in a use case diagram.
- **Use cases:** a use case represents some aspect of functionality of the system, or capability, and is typically representative of some sort of

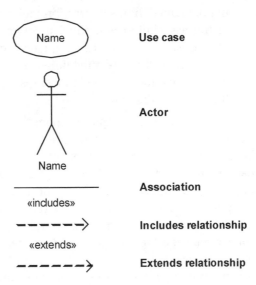

FIGURE 2.18 *Graphical notation for use case diagrams*

requirement of the system. These requirements may be business requirements, functional requirements or non-functional requirements. Use cases, together with actors, represent graphical nodes in the use case diagram.

- **System boundary**: the system boundary, which is represented by a large rectangle in a use case diagram, indicates the divide between the functionality within the system and the actors outside the system. Any diagram that has a system boundary may be thought of as a *context* of the system. Each context of the system represents a view point of the system from a particular stakeholder's point of view and, typically, any system will have a number of contexts defined for it. For example, it is quite common to find a *business context* defined for a system, that represents the high-level business requirements of the organization, as well as a *system context* that represents the individual requirements of a particular project. Also, the *system context* will often be made up of a number of view points, such as the *product context* that represents the requirements of the end product, and the *project context* that represents the requirements for running the projects. All these contexts must be consistent with each other while individually adding value to the understanding of the project. In the case of process modelling, the context defined is known as a 'requirements view' on the process meta-model.

- **Relationships**: there are three basic relationships that are defined in the UML language, which are the *association,* the *includes* dependency and the *extends* dependency. The basic association simply identifies some sort of relationship between an actor and a use case. Unlike conventional associations, associations on use case diagrams should not be named, nor is a direction indicated on them. The actual nature of the association is defined in more detail using UML interaction diagrams, such as the sequence diagram. The two types of dependency that are predefined in the UML are the includes and extends relationships. Relationships represent the graphical paths in the use case diagram.

A use case diagram is unique compared to the other UML diagrams in that it has two specific usages, which are often abused. A use case diagram may be used to model either a context of a system or a set of requirements that has been decomposed from a higher-level requirement and will, ultimately, be traceable back to a context.

Figure 2.19 shows a use case diagram that models a context. The visual indicator that the diagram is a context, rather than a decomposition of some higher-level requirement, is the system boundary, represented by the large rectangle that contains the use cases (ellipses). The actors are outside the boundary of the system and are connected to the use cases by associations. These associations not only relate actors and use cases but

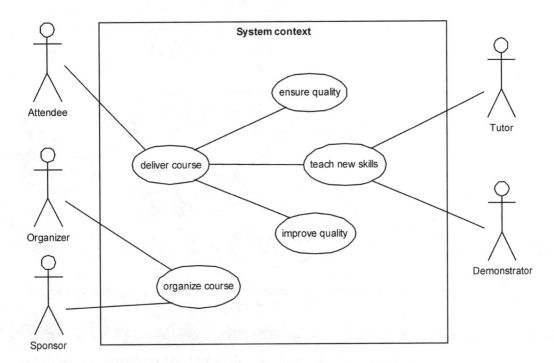

FIGURE 2.19 *Example of a use case diagram showing a context*

each time an association crosses the system boundary, it represents an interface between the system and the outside world.

All use cases in a context should be related to actors outside the system boundary either directly or indirectly. A direct relationship is represented by a dedicated relationship between the use case and one or more actors, whereas as an indirect relationship may be an inherited relationship via a specialization, includes, extends or constrains relationship, described in more detail below.

The other use for the use case diagram is to decompose one of the higher-level requirements into its own diagram. The use case diagram in Figure 2.20 shows the decomposition, or breakdown, of a high-level requirement – in this case the 'organize course' requirement – from the context diagram.

Notice how, in Figure 2.20, the relationships between the use cases have been specified in terms of the special nature of the relationship. There are three basic types of relationship specified within the UML, which are:

- **The specialization relationship**: This is exactly the same as the specialization relationship that is used in class diagrams and, similarly, is read as 'has types'. Therefore, in the diagram, the requirement 'organize course' has two types: 'organize in-house course' and 'organize external course'. The specialization also allows

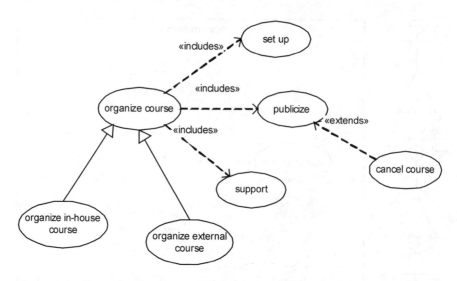

FIGURE 2.20 *Example of a use case diagram showing decomposition of a higher-level requirement*

inheritance, which means that the two child requirements ('organize in-house course' and 'organize external course') both inherit the structure of the parent requirement ('organize course'). Therefore, the three requirements included in the parent requirement are inherited by the two child requirements.

- **The <<includes>> relationship:** the <<includes>> relationship states that any use cases on the directed end of the dashed line are *always* part of the use case on the other end of the line. Therefore, the use case 'organize course' always includes: 'set up', 'publicize' and 'support'. This is how composition is indicated on a use case diagram.

- **The <<extends>> relationship:** the <<extends>> relationship states that any use cases on the directed end of the dashed line are *sometimes* part of the use case on the other end of the line. Therefore, the use case 'cancel course' extends the functionality of the use case 'publicize', depending on certain conditions.

There is a fourth type of relationship that is frequently used in use case diagrams, known as the <<constrains>> relationship. Although not a standard part of the UML notation, the UML is often extended to include such a relationship.

Figure 2.21 shows a <<constrains>> relationship, that is used to relate functional and non-functional requirements together. A functional requirement represents some function of the system into which users or operators are directly inherited, whereas a non-functional requirement represents a requirement that will constrain the way that a functional

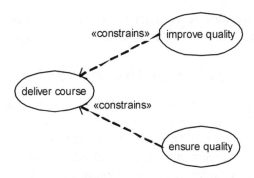

FIGURE 2.21 *The <<constrains>> relationship*

requirement can be realized. In the context of process modelling, non-functional requirements will include requirements such as:

- **Quality requirements**: this will often consist of meeting a particular standard or set of standards. This can be very important and can also be one of the most unrealistic non-functional requirements of a system. It is not uncommon to see well over 50 standards referenced as being 'essential' to the successful implementation of a system. Of course, in reality, it is quite unrealistic to demand that so many standards should be complied with, unless the project is directly related to standards compliance.

- **Implementation requirements**: some non-functional requirements will constrain other requirements by insisting that a particular technique, tool or technology is used as part of the system development. Of course, dictating any of these will limit the way that the system is developed.

- **Environmental requirements**: any system has to operate in some kind of environment, whether it is the natural environment, an artificial environment or whatever. In almost all cases, the type of environment in which the system lives will have some constraining effect on the system.

These non-functional requirements are just as important as the actual functional requirements but can often be far more difficult to quantify and, hence, to validate.

Using use case diagrams for process modelling

Use case diagrams are used to realize the 'requirements view' of the process meta-model, which consists of a number of use case diagrams, each of which represents a context of the system from the viewpoint of one stakeholder or a stakeholder group.

It is often argued that a requirements view is the most important single view of a system, as it is the view to and from which all other views will be traceable. It is crucial, therefore, that the requirements view is both correct and an accurate representation of real life.

CONSISTENCY BETWEEN THE DIAGRAMS

It must be remembered that each of the diagrams is simply a small view of the overall model. This model is a large, complex beast that is difficult to understand. Therefore, breaking the model down into a number of simpler views, each of which is realized visually by a number of diagrams, makes understanding easier. However, in order to have the confidence that the model itself is correct and that our understanding is valid, it is essential that the model is checked for consistency by relating elements of different diagrams together.

The UML is more than just a random collection of drawing elements brought together into a set of diagrams, as every element in the UML is related to another element in some way. These interrelationships are defined in what is known as the *UML meta-model*. The UML meta-model is fully defined in the UML standard (available from www.omg.org) and is, in a nutshell, a UML model of the UML. In order to keep things simple in this book, all relevant consistency relationships have been abstracted into tables in Chapter 4.

CONCLUSIONS

This chapter has presented the basic syntax and notation of four of the 13 UML diagrams that are used for process modelling. The basic concepts have been addressed here generally, but each will be discussed in more detail, with process modelling specifically in mind, in the chapters that follow.

The information presented here is by no means an exhaustive definition of the syntax for each of the UML diagrams, but represents the key elements of each diagram that will be used in the remainder of this book. It is possible to carry out all process modelling activities with this simple notation but, for a more complete description of the UML syntax, semantics and rules, see any of the excellent reference manuals that are generally available (for example, Holt, 2004; Rumbaugh *et al.*, 2004).

3 Requirements for Process Modelling

'Those that don't ask, don't want – those that ask, don't get'

Christine Holt (author's mother)

INTRODUCTION

The previous chapter introduced the UML as the tool that will be used to de-mystify the world of processes. This chapter investigates just why process modelling is so deceptively complex and difficult to get right and identifies a number of problems associated with understanding and communicating processes.

The fact that we are modelling processes means that we are simplifying reality. This means that, by necessity, we will have to miss out some information. A full process specification will consist of the model and an important part of that model is the textual descriptions that accompany all its key elements. This chapter looks at the various requirements for modelling processes effectively and efficiently. Each major point is discussed in the next section.

SPECIFIC PROCESS MODELLING REQUIREMENTS

Complete information

One very real danger that occurs when modelling anything, not just processes, is that too much information may be inadvertently missed out. A process model that is too simplified will not add the amount of value that an appropriately modelled one will and, likewise, a process model containing too much detail will be riddled with complexity and all its associated problems. Reaching the appropriate level of abstraction can be very difficult to achieve, therefore some guidance is required for obtaining the correct level of detail. This is one of the features of the process meta-model that is introduced at the end of this chapter.

Realistic processes

Another problem that occurs with process modelling is one of ensuring the process really reflects the practices carried out in real life. This occurs because processes are usually modelled as abstract notions that are thought about theoretically before being put into practice. This is all well and good, but it is just as important to think about the real-life execution of such processes, which are referred to as 'process instances'; in other words, real-life examples of the processes being executed in the organization.

Process partitioning

Any process model has the potential to contain a very large number of processes and it is important to be able to partition them in some way. The approach to partitioning processes into groups can take many forms. For example, many organizations will take an international standard as the basis for the main process partitions. Rather than using an international standard or best practice model, processes are also often grouped in terms of their functionality, or in terms of areas of responsibility. The actual approach taken will depend on the organization and the nature of the applications of the process, but this decision must be made and recorded in some way.

Process iteration

When processes have been identified and the key features defined, it is important to be able to define how the activities in the process are carried out – the order in which they are executed, the conditions under which they are executed and any timing constraints that may come into play. Very often, the internal workings of a process will be defined as a linear set of activities, whereas, in real life, many processes will exhibit a high degree of iteration. For example, most processes will have decision points and, by the very nature of a decision point, there will be more than one option based on a decision. These different options result in different paths of flow through a process causing a high degree of iteration. Caution must be exercised when identifying iteration, as the more iterations within a diagram, the higher the level of complexity.

In real life, it is possible to execute many instantiations of a single process at the same time. Consider any transaction-processing system where it is a key feature of the system to be able to process transactions in parallel, rather than in a simple sequence.

Complexity and interactions

Interactions exist at many levels in a process model, both in its structural definition and its behaviour. These interactions can be identified visually by looking at the graphical paths (lines) on any diagram that connect the graphical nodes (shapes). It is these relationships and interactions between elements that lead to complexity, rather than the elements themselves. Imagine a set of five elements represented as five classes, as shown in Figure 3.1, which illustrates why relationships and interactions lead to complexity.

First, consider the pattern shown as Figure 3.1a, where there are five classes with no relationships between them. Clearly, this is simple and would be perceived as easy to understand by anyone looking at the shapes, as the level of interaction between the elements (also known as the *coupling*) is zero. This is very often the perception when presented with a text list of things. In reality, however, there are usually relationships between the various elements in a diagram or in a list. This is represented in Figure 3.1b, where each element is now related to the other elements in some way. It is quite clear that Figure 3.1b is more complex than Figure 3.1a. Although both have exactly the same number of elements, in Figure 3.1b the interactions, or the coupling, between these elements is higher than in Figure 3.1a. Finally, consider the case when there are yet more interactions between the same set of elements, as illustrated in Figure 3.1c. Clearly, this is more complex than Figure 3.1b and it is orders of magnitude more complex than Figure 3.1a. Again, it has the same number of elements as Figures 3.1a and b, but the increased number of interactions leads immediately to an increased level of complexity.

Complexity, therefore, is very much a function of the relationships between elements of a diagram, rather than of the number of elements themselves.

A structural diagram has been used in Figure 3.1 – in this case a class diagram – but the same principle applies to any of the diagrams discussed in this book. Also, as these interactions and complex relationships exist on all the different diagrams, they can exist in all views of the system and at all levels of abstraction, for example:

- A very high level of abstraction, such as between the system and the user of the system, or between systems. In terms of process modelling, this manifests itself as requirements for the process.

- A high level of abstraction, such as between subsystems of an overall system, where the elements or components of a system interact to

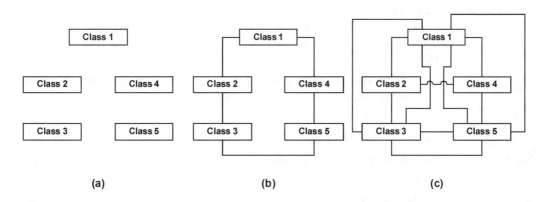

FIGURE 3.1 *The complexity of relationships*

deliver complex behaviour. There will usually be several levels of high abstraction and, in terms of process modelling, this will manifest itself as process executions interacting in different situations.

- A medium level of abstraction, where individual elements are modelled and the interactions represent internal relationships and interactions. In terms of process modelling, this will manifest itself as the definition of the behaviour inside a process.

- A low level of abstraction, where the model represents individual activities, or algorithms, that cannot be decomposed any further. In terms of process modelling, this will manifest itself as defining the behaviour of activities within a process.

When looking at elements within a system, the information is deceptively simple. To get a more realistic view of the system, it is essential to visualize the relationships between these elements.

Traceability

One of the most important goals for any quality system is that of traceability. It is essential to be able to trace from any point of any life cycle back to the original project requirements. For example, during an audit, the auditor may point at any part of the system that is being developed and ask which of the original requirements that part of the system is meeting. The same is true for the process model: it is essential that all the artefacts are not only identified, but that they are also fully traceable. For example, a delegate booking process may require an invoice to be produced and sent out to a customer, but if there is no traceability between the booking process and the associated invoicing process then the whole process will fail.

MEETING THE REQUIREMENTS THROUGH MODELLING

The requirements identified and discussed above can all be met by appropriate use of UML modelling. This section aims to look at each of these requirements and then to relate them to different UML modelling mechanisms to get an idea of how each of them can be visualized using the UML.

We have already seen that a process defines an approach to doing something, therefore there is a clear need to be able to model:

- the name of the process itself;
- the inputs and outputs of the process;
- the activities that are executed in order to achieve the aims of the process.

Another important aspect of process definition is that each of the activities that is identified must also have responsibility defined for it, in terms of a

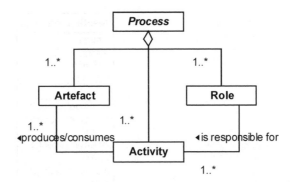

FIGURE 3.2 *Simple definition of a process*

stakeholder role. This information can be represented using a simple class diagram.

Figure 3.2 shows a simple definition of what a process is and how it must be represented. The diagram is read as follows: a 'Process' is made up of one or more 'Role', one or more 'Activity' and one or more 'Artefact'. Also, each 'Activity' produces/consumes one or more 'Artefact' and each 'Role' is responsible for one or more 'Activity'. This is the terminology that will be adopted for the rest of this book.

This diagram is very useful for two reasons:

- It defines the basic structure of the process model itself. This diagram will be expanded later and will form the 'process structure view' in the process meta-model.

- It defines the key terminology to be used throughout the process model. For example, the term 'artefact' has been used here to represent inputs and outputs, but this term could quite easily have been defined as something else, such as 'deliverable', 'work product' or, indeed, 'input' or 'output'. The same is true for the other terms: 'activity' could have been defined as 'task', 'action', and so on, and 'role' could have been defined as 'stakeholder', 'responsibility', and so on.

This diagram is useful for defining the structure and terminology, but it would be impractical to use the same structure to represent *actual* processes, as any process will have a number of activities, artefacts and stakeholders, each of which would be represented by a class on a diagram like this one. Therefore, the diagram is simplified by representing the whole process as a single class. Remembering back to the UML element of the class, a class can be further described by a number of attributes and a number of operations. An attribute describes a feature of a class, which is comparable to the artefacts of a process. Likewise, an operation describes something that is done in a class, which is comparable to the activities in a process. Therefore, it is possible to represent a process, together with its

47

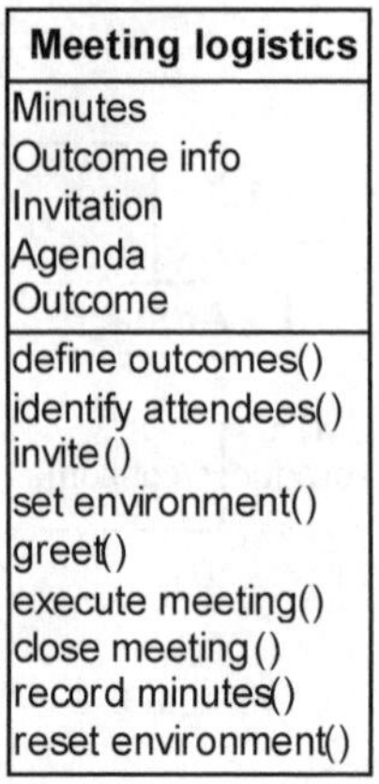

Meeting logistics
Minutes
Outcome info
Invitation
Agenda
Outcome
define outcomes()
identify attendees()
invite ()
set environment()
greet()
execute meeting()
close meeting ()
record minutes()
reset environment()

FIGURE 3.3 *Compact definition of a process*

artefacts and activities, as a single class that exhibits attributes and operations.

Figure 3.3 shows a class that represents the process 'Meeting logistics', which is executed in order to plan and run meetings. The name of the class is the name of the process, in this case 'Meeting logistics'. The attribute names, shown in the second box, represent the names of the artefacts that are produced and consumed as part of the process. The operation names, shown in the third box, represent the activity names that are the individual steps in the process that produce and consume the artefacts.

So far, the information on the diagram has shown two of the three things that need to be specified – the artefacts and the activities – but has not shown the stakeholders. The stakeholders can be represented on a different class diagram, but one that is dedicated to identifying the stakeholders as classes and the relationships between them. This class diagram represents a stakeholder view of the system and forms part of the process meta-model.

TAILORING PROCESSES

No matter how well understood a process is, how often it is used or how well specified it is, processes always need to be tailored. Tailoring a process means specializing it in some way, which could be for any number of reasons:

- **A natural evolution of the process due to change in internal process requirements**: All processes must be reviewed periodically to ensure that they are still fit for purpose. As time goes on, the process itself may evolve in terms of the way that it is being implemented by the people in the organization. Perhaps a new software tool is being used that makes the process easier to follow by automating one or more of the steps. In such a case, the process must be revisited and re-verified.

- **A natural evolution of the process due to a change in the organizational requirements of the process**: in many instances, the process must evolve due to a change inside the organization. Maybe the business of the organization has evolved and the processes need to be checked to make sure that they meet the new requirements – in other words, validation. For example, consider a company that suddenly starts to create real-time or safety-critical systems which previously had only been involved in basic systems. Although the original process itself still works (verification), it no longer meets the organization's new requirements (validation).

- **A forced evolution of the process (change in external requirements)**: As well as the internal, organizational requirements for a process changing, there can also be external, or outside, influences that affect the process. For example, there may be a change in law, best practice standards, and so on, that will impact on the product associated with the process, or the process itself directly, which means that the process may have to be tailored in some way. For example, consider the case of electro-magnetic compatibility (EMC) regulations that now affect just about every electronic product on the market. It is no longer good enough to make an excellent TV set, for example; if the TV set does not meet the EMC regulations, then it cannot be sold – regardless of how it may be perceived to be. In such a case, the processes must be checked against external requirements (validation) even though the process itself still functions as was originally intended (verification).

- **New applications/projects**: As time goes on, any organization will evolve in terms of the way that it operates, the products that it produces, and so on. As the organization evolves, then so must the products. For example, an organization involved with developing mobile phones may branch out into personal electronic organizers, which would result in the processes needing to be validated once more.

- **Off-the-shelf process**: The process may be an off-the-shelf process that can be bought from a specialist company, such as the content of a book or standard or, in some cases, a shrink-wrapped product. Any predefined process will invariably not meet every requirement of any organization. Such an off-the-shelf process is an excellent basis for a bespoke process model but, as is the inherent nature of any bespoke system, it must be tailored to meet specialized requirements. Every organization or business unit within an organization will have its own specialized requirements. Even organizations that look on the surface as if they are very similar will have some differences and it is these differences that cause many of the headaches associated with processes. In fact, many of these off-the-shelf solution providers are very open about what their processes can and cannot do and they are, indeed, sold as a small part of an overall package that includes specialist consultancy and tailoring services provided by the vendor. The danger arises, however, when the vendor is so arrogant as to claim that their product, in its off-the-shelf form, will meet all the requirements of any potential customer organization. (Remember that this book states, quite explicitly, in Chapter 1 and in later chapters, that the process meta-model provided as the cornerstone of the book must be tailored to meet the needs of an organization – which is one of the reasons for this section.)

There is a need, therefore, to be able to tailor a process to meet changing requirements or an evolution of the organization or business. Any process that is represented by a single class in UML can be tailored very easily, as there is a basic mechanism in the UML for tailoring a class, known as *specialization.* Specializing a class, is, in effect, tailoring that class for a specific usage.

Consider a process that is defined in terms of its artefacts and activities, represented in UML by a class with attributes and operations. This process may be intended to be appropriate for a specific type of project, but what happens when the requirements change?

Figure 3.4 shows an example system design process where the artefacts and activities are represented by attributes and operations respectively. This process may very well have been used for some time within the organization and may have been used very successfully. However, what would happen if the requirements for the process were to change? For example, the requirements for producing architecture will differ quite significantly if the architecture is for a real-time system or a safety-critical system. In such cases, there is a need for additional information to be

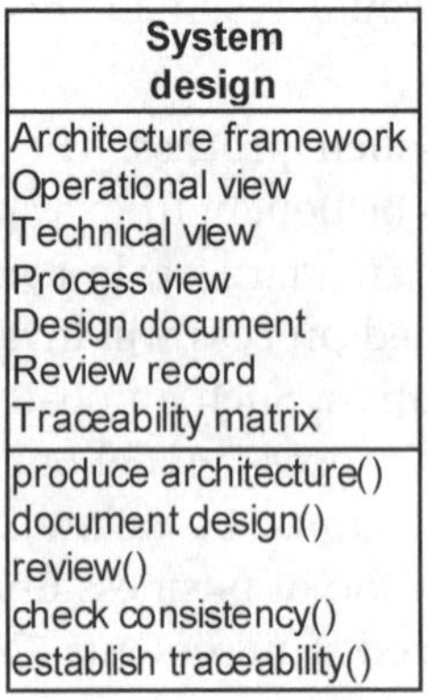

System design
Architecture framework
Operational view
Technical view
Process view
Design document
Review record
Traceability matrix
produce architecture()
document design()
review()
check consistency()
establish traceability()

FIGURE 3.4 *Example process: 'System design'*

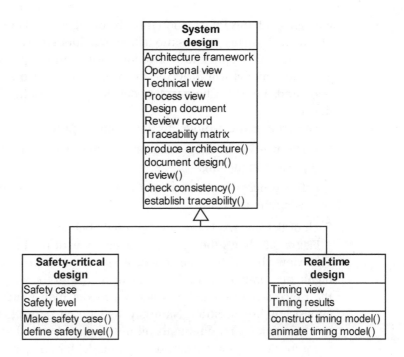

FIGURE 3.5 *Tailored processes*

added to the basic process. Maybe more artefacts are required, such as a safety case in the example of the safety-critical systems, which will also result in the definition of an additional activity to generate the safety case. The specialization mechanism in the UML allows exactly this sort of tailoring to be defined.

Figure 3.5 shows how the specialization mechanism can be used to tailor a basic process by adding in extra artefacts and activities in its tailored child class. Note that, because of the rules of inheritance, all the existing artefacts and activities for the basic 'System design' process will be inherited by the child classes of 'Safety-critical design' and 'Real-time design'. Also note that, as the behaviour of the process has been changed (more operations, hence activities, have been added), the process requires a new behavioural view to specify exactly how the new activities behave within the process.

This specialization mechanism allows any process to be tailored so that this new information can be retained within the process model.

THE PROCESS META-MODEL

The requirements for process modelling have been discussed together with how each of them may be realized using the UML. However, this is still not

51

enough, as all this information must be brought together in a format that is of practical use for process modelling practitioners. This bringing together of different concepts and realizations results in the process meta-model. This meta-model will form the main discussion for the remainder of the book and, indeed, Chapter 4 is devoted to describing each element in detail.

The process meta-model has two main aspects:

- **The process concept view**: shows the main concepts involved with process modelling.

- **The process realization view**: shows how to realize these concepts using the UML.

Each of these views is introduced briefly below.

Figure 3.6 shows the process concept view of the process meta-model. This view shows the main concepts involved in process modelling and highlights some of the problems associated with the subject. The whole of the process meta-model is a generic model that is intended for use by almost any organization. Naturally, as with all things generic, it will not meet everyone's requirements all of the time, but will serve as a starting point for developing a bespoke meta-model for any particular industry or organization. For example, it is often the case that the terminology used here will be inappropriate, depending on the industry or organization, or that there already exists a well-known set of terms for process modelling. In many cases, although the actual words on the process meta-model change, the pattern of the meta-model (the layout of the shapes on the

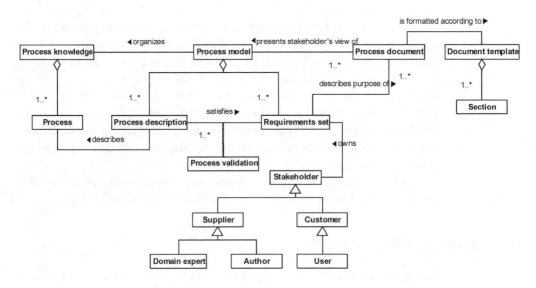

FIGURE 3.6 *Process meta-model: Process concept view*

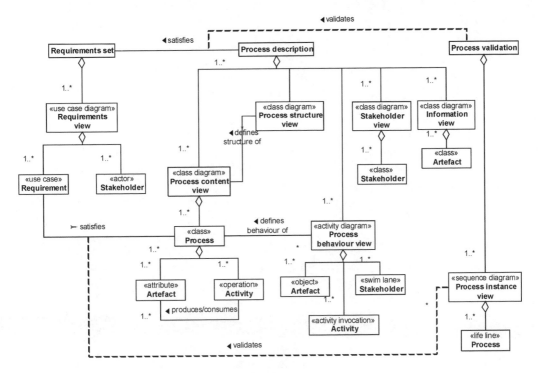

FIGURE 3.7 *Process realization view*

page) stays largely unchanged. This diagram is discussed in depth in Chapter 4.

Figure 3.7 shows how the concepts from Figure 3.6 may be realized using the UML. Each concept has been broken down into more detail and UML modelling concepts associated with each one.

This process meta-model, when viewed in its entirety, forms a practical yet very effective tool when it comes to modelling any sort of processes in real life.

CONCLUSIONS

This chapter introduced a set of practical requirements for process modelling that must be met before a correct and robust process model can be specified. Each of these requirements may be realized by using effective modelling – in the case of this book, the modelling notation adopted is the UML. By bringing all this information together, it is possible to specify a process meta-model that not only identifies the key concepts involved with process modelling, but also specifies how each one may be realized using the UML.

Chapter 4 takes a detailed look at the process meta-model and how it can be used for practical and effective process modelling.

4 The Process Meta-Model Expanded

'Da dah, da da da dah, da da da da da-da-da-da, da da da-da-da-da-DAH-DAH'
Theme tune to *The Magnificent Seven*, UA/Mirsch-Alpha

INTRODUCTION

The secret of any card trick relies on the fact that the audience is presented with only a single view of the trick – the one that they are intended to see. What the audience does not see is the preparation, the set-up, the confederates in the crowd, the sleight-of-hand, the sneak glimpses and the general deception employed by the magician. In order to understand such a trick, it is important to look at it from many different angles, or viewpoints. The same is true of process modelling: the secret is to look at any process from a number of different views – the number being seven. The views, when combined, form the process meta-model.

The concept of the meta-model has been introduced in previous chapters and this chapter provides a full description of the process meta-model. A meta-model is, quite simply, a model of a model. Therefore, the process meta-model is a model of a model that is used for process modelling. The process meta-model itself has two views:

- **The process concept view**: shows the key concepts associated with process modelling and draws relationships between them.
- **The process realization view**: shows how the conceptual view may be realized using the modelling techniques introduced in this book. This realization view is indispensable as, among other things, it serves as a checklist when specifying and analysing processes.

The next section describes the process meta-model in more detail. The following two sections then look at ensuring consistency in a process model and give some example uses of how the meta-model may be used to add value to a process modelling exercise.

PROCESS CONCEPT VIEW

This section provides an overview of the process concept view (see Figure 4.1).

Figure 4.1 shows the process concept view. To begin with, we consider the diagram and the concepts that it conveys. These are are then used as a basis for discussion.

In the top-left corner of the diagram, there is a class named 'Process knowledge' that is made up of one or more 'Process'. This process knowledge and its associated processes represent any sort of process knowledge whatsoever, in its raw form. For example, this process knowledge may be tacit knowledge inside someone's head that may need to be extracted in order to understand it properly. Otherwise, it may be written down in a book or process document. Basically, this process knowledge could be almost any sort of information relating to processes.

On the right-hand-side of the diagram, there is a class named 'Process document' and an associated class named 'Document template'. The process document class here represents the final manifestation of the process definition in some sort of document. This could be a standard, procedure or work practice, which could be a hard-copy document, electronic copy (such as a word-processing file) or some sort of web-based document. This document is formatted according to the document template, which will probably reflect some in-house or corporate style for document presentation. This document template is made up of a number of specific sections, subsections, and so on, represented on the model simply as the class 'Section'.

Between the raw process knowledge and the final, deliverable process document lies the 'Process model' and it is this process model that represents an ordered, structured and consistent representation of the

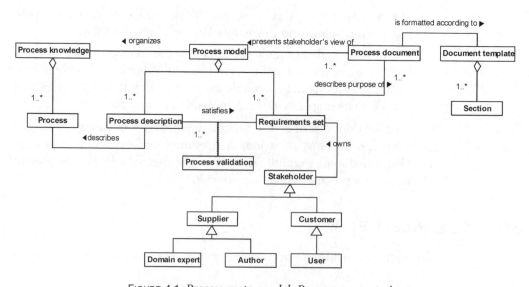

FIGURE 4.1 *Process meta-model: Process concept view*

process knowledge. The process document is based directly on this process model.

In fact, it is possible to redraw the same diagram but, this time, to group the diagram into three main sets of information, as shown in Figure 4.2.

The main discussion point for the diagram in Figure 4.1 is the relationship or, more to the point, the lack of relationship, between the source information in the form of the process knowledge and the presentation of the output, in the form of the process document. This is the most contentious point on the diagram, but is also the most important.

Problems with processes have been discussed previously in this book, and this lack of relationship represents one of the biggest and most common of these problems. There is *no* direct relationship between the two. When there is a direct relationship, then this is where the major problems start to occur. The source information is raw, disorganized and often chaotic information contained in someone's head or in a document that exhibits the three classic 'evils of life':

- **Complexity**: as the information is unstructured, it is very easy to hide or overlook complexity. As mentioned in Chapter 3, it is the relationships between things that cause complexity.

- **Lack of understanding**: very often, the source information is poorly understood and, therefore, prone to error. Even processes that work very well are often misunderstood and, hence, not very robust to change or tailoring.

- **Poor communication**: if the process knowledge exists within some- one's head, it is often very difficult for them to communicate this information to someone else, particularly if the process knowledge is something that someone does every day and has become a part of them. The same is true for written information, where badly written text can lead to problems of both complexity and lack of under- standing.

The document template is often perceived as the answer to these three problems but, as is often the case, these templates can be a pain rather than a boon:

- **Complexity**: although many people see templates as a way to simplify a document, the headings are often too generic and can lead to people putting information anywhere, particularly if the information that they want to record is not a direct fit for any of the headings. Also, people will tend to be driven by the headings and simply pour all their process knowledge under each heading, rather than thinking about what they are writing.

- **Lack of understanding**: many people assume that because something is well set out (it has headings), the information is correct. By simply following a template, it is very easy for people to not think about what they are writing. One advantage of an approach such as the meta-model approach is that it forces people to think about what they are doing and makes it far more difficult to gloss over tough issues and decisions.

- **Poor communication**: a poorly thought-out template can easily communicate the wrong information or lead to a false sense of security, as suggested in the previous two points. One common problem is that many templates are based on other templates, which results in the same information being generated for different types of artefact. It is crucial that the appropriate information is communicated by each artefact in the system.

Another key element of this diagram is the relationship between 'Process document' and the 'Requirements set' and, in particular, the numbering ratio between the two. Note that the diagram reads as: each 'Requirements set' describes the purpose of *one or more* 'Process document'. It is the 'one or more' that is of specific interest here. It is quite often the case where different process documents, for example, standards, are produced based on the same information. Bear in mind that the diagram also says that the 'Process document' presents a stakeholder's view of the 'Process model', which means that each stakeholder has their own view on the process model. Imagine, for example, a process model that describes the processes involved with using a rail system. Although it is a single system, the processes for, say, a passenger compared to those of a driver will be completely different. Therefore, the same set of processes in the 'Process description' may represent a completely different 'Requirements set' for each stakeholder. Therefore, it is possible for a single process model to be realized in a number of process documents that, although based on the same source information, will represent a different stakeholder's point of view.

Figure 4.2 shows exactly the same information as Figure 4.1, except, this time, the information has been grouped into three main headings:

- **Source**: represents any raw process information.
- **Understanding**: a grouping that represents the model of all the process knowledge and forms the basis for the final document.
- **Presentation**: a grouping that represents the final presentation of the process model, such as a standard, a procedure, and so on.

Therefore, to summarize, the 'Source' information is the raw process knowledge, the 'Understanding' represents the ordered, structured and consistent model of this information and, finally, the 'Presentation' represents the final manifestation of the process knowledge.

The 'Source' information is out there in the real world and can be obtained from any number of sources. The 'Presentation information' is the intended output of a process generation exercise, whereas the

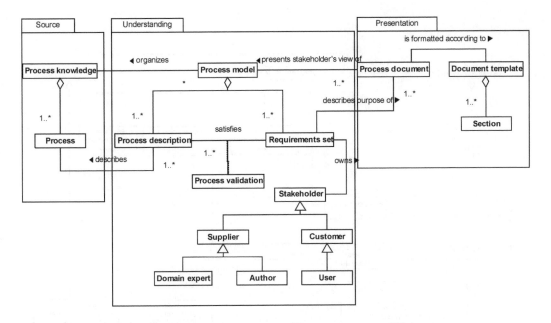

FIGURE 4.2 *Process concept view with groupings*

'Understanding' forms the focus of this book. This 'Understanding' information, in the form of the process meta-model, is expanded upon in subsequent sections of this chapter.

PROCESS REALIZATION VIEW

This section introduces the process realization view and describes each of its part in detail. An example is used throughout to illustrate what each of the different views should look like. Also, of critical importance is the concept of consistency between the different views and this is dealt with in the next section. Following this, a discussion on the uses of this meta-model is presented together with some typical scenarios that demonstrate practical uses for these techniques.

The process realization view shows how the information introduced by the process concept view may be modelled using the UML. This section looks at each of the main elements of the process model in more detail. This is then related to the UML and the different elements of the language that may be used for each part of the realization view.

Figure 4.3 shows the process realization view, in which the main elements of the process model introduced in Figure 4.1 are broken down into further detail. In this diagram, a new modelling element has been introduced – that of UML *stereotypes*. A stereotype is a way of tailoring the UML language for a particular application; in this case the language has been tailored to relate UML concepts to the process modelling concepts.

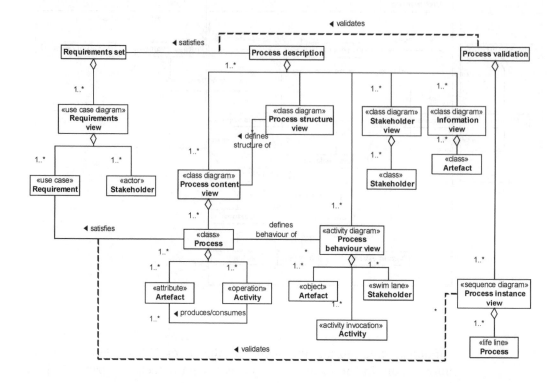

FIGURE 4.3 *Process realization view*

Any class that has words written above it in chevrons <<>> is not a regular UML class, but is known as a UML stereotype. In Figure 4.3, whenever there is a class name with a word in chevrons written above it, the word in chevrons represents the element of the UML language used to realize the concept represented by the class. For example, the concept of a 'Requirements view' (indicated by the class 'Requirements view') is realized in UML using a use case diagram (indicated by <<use case diagram>>).

A complete set of these views is required for a full specification of any process – the omission of any single view can lead to problems. There are some situations where not all views are required, but these situations usually relate to process models that are deliberately incomplete. For example, most international standards will specify 'what' to do, but not 'how'. This results in a subset of the views being produced with an emphasis on structure rather than behaviour. However, even in situations such as these, it is still often the case that all views, including the behavioural views, need to be considered in order to get the subset of the views correct. This is discussed in more detail later in this chapter.

There are seven views in the process meta-model: the requirements view, the process structure view, the process content view, the stakeholder view, the information view, the process instance view and the process behaviour view. Each of these views is now discussed in more detail.

THE SEVEN VIEWS OF THE META-MODEL

The requirements view

The requirements view specifies the overall aims of the process document and is realized, in the UML, by a use case diagram. It is possible to have a number of different requirements views for a single process model, depending on the number of stakeholders involved. Typically, each process document is aimed at a particular set of stakeholders and each one of these stakeholder sets has its own requirements set. Theoretically, it is possible for every stakeholder in the system to have their own process document, written specifically for them, but this is impractical in terms of the sheer number of process documents required, so the process documents are almost always geared towards groups of stakeholders, rather than individuals.

The requirements view is also very important as it forms the basis for validating each process. It is quite often the case that a set of processes is defined that is fully verified, but that is not validated. The difference between the two is defined, for the purposes of this book, as follows:

- **Process verification**: concerned with ensuring that the process works properly – that it is correct, consistent and will respond to a set of inputs in a predictable fashion.

- **Process validation**: more subtle than process verification, as process validation asks whether the process actually achieves what it is supposed to. It is perfectly possible for a process model to be correct and working (verified) but not to meet the requirements for the process model, in which case the process model is useless.

It is the requirements view that provides an understanding of exactly why the process model is needed in the first place. If the requirements for the process model are not known, then how on earth can a process model be validated? The answer, of course, is that validation is impossible without an understanding of what the requirements are.

One of the features of a robust process model is its ability to remain valid over a long period of time. In order to do this, the process model must evolve to react to the changing environment in which it lives. As time goes on, changes will occur in the surrounding environment, so it is important that this can be captured in some way, and it is the requirements view that achieves this. Examples of changes include:

- **Changes in related process models**: invariably, a process model does not exist in isolation and has to co-exist with a number of other process models, such as related standards, procedures, and so on. It is quite possible, and, indeed, quite common, for these external process models to change in some way and to render elements of the actual process model redundant, incorrect or simply out of date.

- **Changes in the business**: businesses are living entities and, as such, are subject to change due to any number of factors, such as technology changes, best practice changes, new business areas opening up, automation of production, and so on. As the business evolves, then so must the process model to reflect this.

These changes are nothing new but, in many instances, they often go unnoticed as the process model still functions in a correct fashion, but it can no longer meet its new requirements. This is analogous to verification and validation:

- *Verification* means that something works correctly and without problems. Clearly, it is important that any process model can be verified.
- *Validation* means that something does what it is supposed to do or, to put it another way, that it meets its requirements. Clearly, it is also important that any process model can be validated.

It is the combination of these two, however, that delivers a good process model, as it is quite common for a process model to be verified and validated when it is first defined. However, as time goes on, the requirements change, as discussed above, which leads to a non-validated, yet still verified process model. It is the fact that the process model remains verified that leads to complacency. Therefore, it is crucial that any process model is continuously assessed on a regular basis, maybe once or twice per year, in order to make sure that the requirements for the process model are still accurate and that the process model itself can be validated against these requirements.

The requirements view, therefore, is essential for ensuring that the process model is correct and can be validated over a period of time, and that it evolves to reflect any changes in the environment.

Figure 4.4 shows an example requirements view for an invoicing process. The main requirements for the view are shown visually by the use cases and the related stakeholders are shown by actors outside the boundary of the system. Each time there is a relationship identified between a use case and one or more stakeholders this signifies that an interface exists between the process and the stakeholders.

In this example, the main requirement is to 'Ensure payment', which includes four lower-level requirements:

- 'Raise invoice', which represents generating the invoice.
- 'Check', which represents the requirement for ensuring that all the invoice details are correct – bearing in mind that incorrect invoices do not get paid.

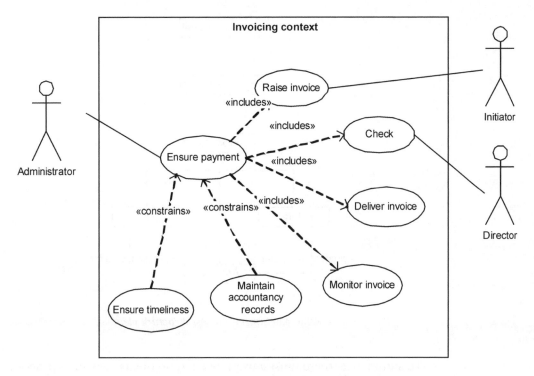

FIGURE 4.4 *Example requirements view for an invoicing process*

- 'Deliver invoice', which represents the requirement for making sure that the invoice gets to the right person and place.
- 'Monitor invoice', which represents the requirement for continuously checking the progress of the invoice through the customer's invoicing process.

Note that there are also two large constraints on the main requirement, which are:

- 'Ensure timeliness', which makes sure that invoices are paid on time.
- 'Maintain accountancy records', which restricts the main requirement in that however the requirements are met, there must be an established audit trail.

Consider now how these requirements may change over time. For example, an additional constraint may be added that relates to using a particular accountancy methodology (such as accrual or pre-payment accounting for VAT) or tool. Requirements may also change because of problems or ambiguities with the current process. For example, it may become an issue that the checking requirement needs to be carried out by someone independent of creating the invoice, or maybe specifically someone at, say, director level. All of these subtleties must be built into the requirements view if they are major concerns for the process.

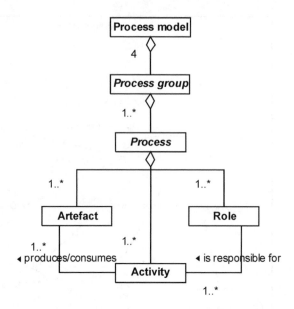

FIGURE 4.5 *Simple process structure view*

To summarize, there must always be a requirements view for a process. A process without any defined requirements may be verified but will *never be validated.*

The process structure view

The process structure view shows a high-level representation of the basic structure of, and the terminology used throughout, the process and is realized using a class diagram. This view only needs to be generated once and then it will dictate the basic structure of all the subsequent processes.

Typical decisions that need to be made here include obtaining a consensus on the terminology to be used throughout the project and identifying the high-level classifications, or groupings, of processes.

This view is very useful for mapping between different process models at a high level, resulting in a basic correlation between the terminology used between process models, which can be invaluable when it comes to audits and assessments. This is explored fully in Chapter 5, which is concerned with process mapping and metrics.

The process structure view is realized using a class diagram in the UML, with each class representing one of the main concepts within the standard, an example of which is shown in Figure 4.5.

Figure 4.5 shows a simple process structure view that defines the key terminology to be used in the example process model. It can be seen that the 'Process model' is made up of four 'Process group', each of which is made up of one or more 'Process'. Each 'Process' is made up of one or more 'Artefact', one or more 'Activity' and one or more 'Role'.

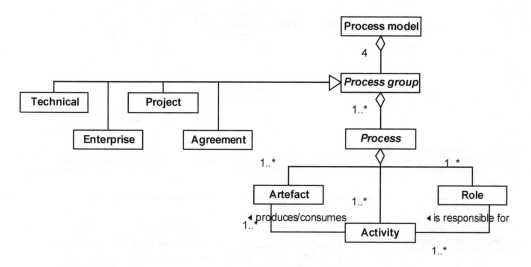

FIGURE 4.6 *More detailed process structure view, highlighting types of 'Process group'*

Furthermore, each 'Role' is responsible for one or more 'Activity' and each 'Activity' produces/consumes one or more 'Artefact'.

Therefore, the basic terminology, together with the relationships between the terms has been identified and can be used as the basis for the process model glossary. This is the terminology that will be used throughout this book, as the view has already contributed to the understanding of process modelling.

It is also possible to add more detail to this view; for example, Figure 4.5 identifies four different types of 'Process group' but there is no indication of what these groups are. Therefore, a more detailed view may be produced.

Figure 4.6 shows a more detailed process structure view, this time with the additional definitions concerning the process groups. In this view, the

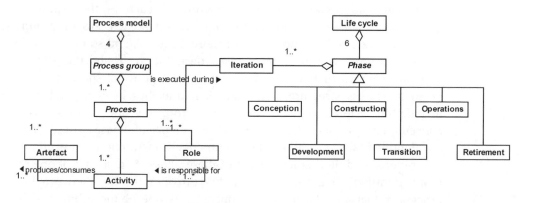

FIGURE 4.7 *More detailed process structure view, highlighting life cycle concepts*

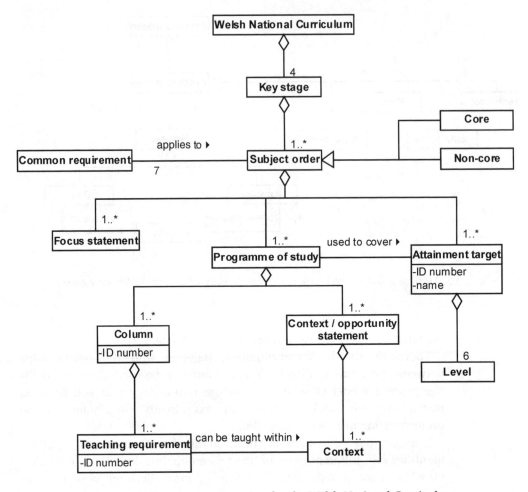

FIGURE 4.8 *Process structure view for the Welsh National Curriculum*

four types of process group are identified as: 'Enterprise', 'Project', 'Technical' and 'Agreement'. The structure of each of these process groups is the same – they all inherit the structure of each 'Process group' and hence each is made up of one or more 'Process', and so on.

It is also possible and, in most cases, desirable to expand the process structure view to include life cycle concepts. Figure 4.7 shows a more detailed process structure view that, this time, has been expanded to include life cycle concepts. It can be seen from this view that there is a concept of a 'Life cycle' that is made up of six types of 'Phase'. These types are identified as: 'Conception', 'Development', 'Construction', 'Transition', 'Operations' and 'Retirement'. Each of these phases is made up of one or more 'Iteration'. It is this iteration that provides the link between the process model and the life cycle concepts, as one or more 'Process' is executed over each 'Phase'.

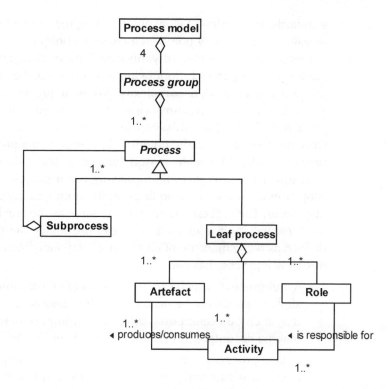

FIGURE 4.9 *Example of a potentially dangerous process structure view*

The types of process group have not been shown in Figure 4.7, purely to make the diagram easier to read. Indeed, although it is possible to amalgamate Figures 4.6 and 4.7 into a single diagram, it is often easier to communicate this information by splitting the diagram into two, or three, smaller views that are consistent with one another.

In some cases, the process structure view can be relatively simple, yet in others the view can be quite complex. As an example of this, the model in Figure 4.8 shows the process structure view for the Welsh National Curriculum which is the standard for education in Wales. This process structure view contains many concepts and is, in comparison to Figure 4.5, relatively complex.

It is interesting to note that, in the UK, there exist several standards for school education, all of which fall under the banner of the *National Curriculum* but each of which has a slight difference in content. For example, in Wales, there is a subject order for learning the Welsh language, which does not exist in the English version of the standard, but that is in the *content* of the standard rather than the structure of the standard, as illustrated in Figure 4.8. In fact, the process structure view for both variations on the standard are *identical*, except for the name of the standard itself. The ability to be able to compare and contrast different standards from different view points, using the meta-model, can be quite revealing and is a very powerful analysis technique.

There is another reason why this view is particularly powerful that is not immediately apparent from looking at Figures 4.5, 4.6 and 4.7 and this is the concept of hidden complexity. When a process model is defined without a process structure view, it is very easy to over-decompose processes. To illustrate this, consider Figure 4.9, which shows a process structure view that has the potential to lead to many problems within the process model. The main reason for this is that this model shows the situation where it is possible to decompose a process into a number of subprocesses and there is no limit on the number of decompositions that may occur. The process structure is the same as the one in Figure 4.5 until the 'Process' itself is defined. Whereas previously the process had been defined as being made up of one or more 'Artefact', 'Activity' and 'Role', in this view a process has two types:

- A 'Subprocess', which can be made up of one or more 'Process', which allows a process to be decomposed into another level of detail, which may then be decomposed into another level of detail which, in turn, may be decomposed into another level, and so on.

- A 'Leaf process', which is the lowest level of decomposition permitted in this structure and, hence, is made up of one or more 'Artefact', one or more 'Activity' and one or more 'Role'.

The danger exists here because it is possible to have one set of processes that can be decomposed over many, many levels, whereas other processes are not. This unevenness of the process decomposition often leads to an imbalance of the process model and can lead to processes either being too high level or overly detailed. A possible solution, in this case, would be to impose restrictions on the number of levels permitted that would avoid this problem. This process structure is redeemable, although potentially dangerous, whereas the example in Figure 4.10 is simply downright dangerous.

Notice that the difference between Figure 4.10 and Figure 4.9 is simply where the definition of the artefacts, activities and roles lies. In this case, it is possible to define roles, artefacts and activities for a subprocess as well as a leaf process – as the structure of the class 'Process' is inherited to both 'Subprocess' and 'Leaf process'. This leads to the very real possibility that a subprocess may be defined in terms of its activities and artefacts and *in addition to this specification* the subprocess may then be further decomposed into many other nested levels of process definition. This is a surprisingly common mistake to make and all but destroys any consistency in a process model.

When defining a process structure view, it is essential to think about how many levels of nesting or decomposition are required and then to specify this explicitly in this view.

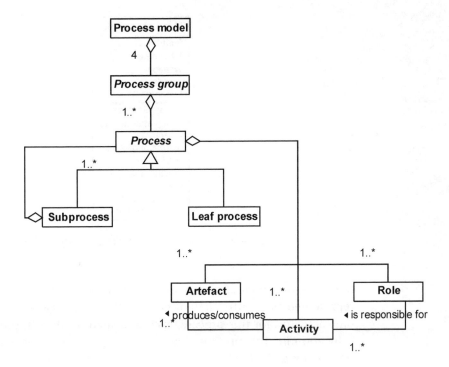

FIGURE 4.10 *Example of a dangerous process structure view*

The process content view

The process content view shows the actual content, in terms of activities and artefacts, by representing each process as a single class. Due to the large number of processes within an organization, it is usual to produce a process content view for each classification, or process grouping, from the process structure view. Consider, for instance, the example that was used in Figure 4.6 that identified four types of process category. In this case, it is far more practical to produce four process content views – one for each process category – rather than trying to fit all processes onto a single diagram.

The process content view is realized in UML by a class diagram, and is very closely related to the process structure view in that it is the process content view that shows the *actual* activities and artefacts (adopting the terminology from Figure 4.5) exhibited by each process. Each process has a class to represent it and the process artefacts are represented by class attributes, whereas the process activities are represented by class operations. An example of this is shown in Figure 4.11.

Figure 4.11 shows an example of a process expressed in the notation described above. In this view, the process to be described is called 'Meeting logistics' and is intended to describe the set-up and running of a meeting within an organization. The name of the process is expressed as

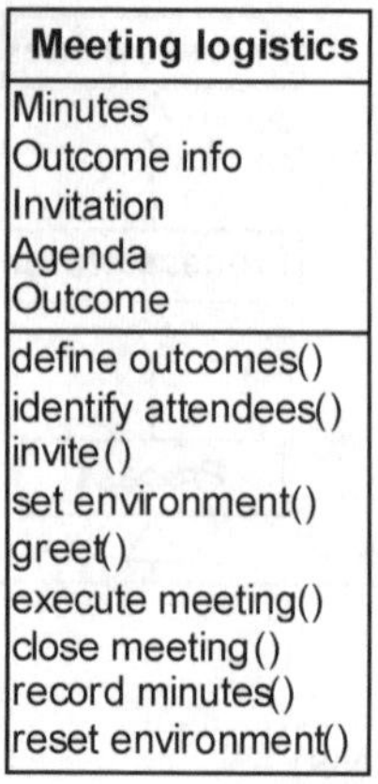

Meeting logistics
Minutes
Outcome info
Invitation
Agenda
Outcome
define outcomes()
identify attendees()
invite()
set environment()
greet()
execute meeting()
close meeting()
record minutes()
reset environment()

FIGURE 4.11 *Process content view: Example process*

the name of the class. There are five artefacts for this process, each one represented as an attribute on the class 'Meeting logistics'. There are also nine activities for this process, each indicated by an operation.

By adopting this presentation style, it is possible to represent an entire process by a single class, while showing all of its artefacts and activities. This notation is not only simple and concise, but also allows an idea of the complexity of each process to be ascertained, albeit at a very high level, simply by looking at the number of attributes and operations and the ratio of their numbers. Consider the processes described in Figure 4.12, which shows a more-populated process content view showing the higher-level framework of the process model that has been abstracted from the process structure view. The process group 'Enterprise' is made up of a number of processes, three of which are: 'Tender application', 'Staff appraisal' and 'Customer invoice'.

An ideal, well-balanced process should contain about seven attributes and operations. This is because the number of things that a human can remember at any one time is defined as seven, plus or minus two – quite by coincidence, this is also the number of views in the process meta-model. Bearing this simple rule in mind, there are a number of issues with the three processes presented here:

- **Too many activities**: if a process exists with far more than nine (seven plus two) activities, such as the 'Tender application' process in Figure 4.12, the chance of someone being able to understand this process begins to diminish as the number of activities increases. There are simply too many steps involved in this task, which will, potentially, lead to complexity when the process is executed (this is discussed in more detail below in 'The process behaviour view'). This high number could be due to the fact that the activities represent very small steps of activity, which means that the level of granularity of the activities

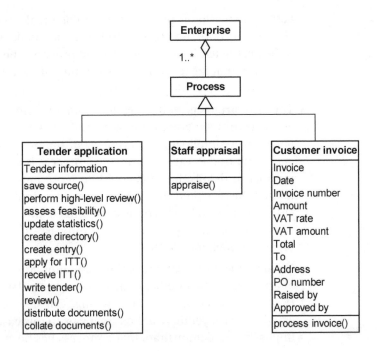

FIGURE 4.12 *Process content view: Warning signs*

should be changed so that fewer activities represent the same behaviour. This high number could also be due to the fact that there is simply too much going on in this single process, and maybe the process should be broken down into two or more simpler processes that describe the same behaviour. Which of these two reasons is the cause will become more apparent when we examine another view – the process behaviour view – for this process.

- **Too many artefacts**: the same principles can be applied when the number of artefacts, represented by attributes, is excessive. An excessive number of artefacts (represented by attributes) may be due to the fact that the individual artefacts are too detailed and that the level of granularity of information needs to be raised. For example, in the 'Customer invoice' process, many of the attributes could be represented by a single artefact, which would decrease the number of overall artefacts.

- **Too few activities**: the situation where the number of activities defined is very low, typically one or two, can mean one of three things. First, the activities are identified at a very high level. In the example in Figure 4.12, the 'Customer invoice' process has a single activity identified named 'Process invoice'. This is practically useless as it does not convey enough information about the steps involved in processing the invoice – it would be just as easy to write 'execute process' as the activity name in all processes and hence make the whole model far simpler. Second, the process itself may be too detailed and may need to be abstracted into another, related process. The third possibility is, of course, that the diagram is correct, but this is quite unlikely, bearing in mind the first two possibilities.

- **Too few artefacts**: following on from the previous point, too few artefacts result in exactly the same problems but, this time, the danger lies in over-simplifying the artefacts of the process. For example, the end result of the 'Customer invoice' process is a single invoice with a number of details, but this could be represented as a single artefact named 'Invoice' and the diagram greatly simplified. However, in this case, the process has become so simplified and over-abstracted that it is no longer adding value to the process model and, hence, the organizational knowledge.

- **No activities or no artefacts**: if the situation arises where the number of artefacts or the number of activities is zero, alarm bells should start to go off immediately. This is wrong. Consider the situation where activities exist, yet there are no artefacts. In this case it means that it is impossible to demonstrate that a process has been executed – there is no evidence identified for any of its activity execution. Also, consider the situation where there are artefacts but no activities – where do the artefacts come from? It may be that the artefacts are part of a data store, in which case the owner class is not a process, but some sort of *storage element*. It should be noted here that it is possible to have a process grouping or classification in UML that has neither artefacts nor activities but, again, this is not a process as such.

- **Out of balance ratio**: considering the ratio of the artefacts to activities on the class is a quick, yet often accurate way to judge how well balanced a process is. Although there are no hard rules for this, an ideal process should have between five and nine of both artefacts and activities. It is also possible to gain an appreciation of how well thought-out a process is by looking at the ratio.

The process content view encapsulates all of the processes that exist within the process model and, therefore, gives a good overview of the scope of the capability of an organization in the various process groups.

The process behaviour view

The process content view identifies all the processes of interest for a system. For each of these processes, the activities and artefacts are also identified. In terms of modelling, the process content view is a structural view of the process and, therefore, there must be a corresponding behavioural aspect of the model. One of the views in the behavioural aspect of the model is the process behaviour view, which describes the behaviour, or the *how*, of a single process. Remembering the rules of UML, any class that exhibits behaviour (has operations) must have an activity diagram to describe its behaviour. As the process content view has already identified a number of processes that are represented as classes, and each of theses classes has at least one operation, then it follows that each of these classes must have an associated behavioural view. This means that each process from the process content view will have a process behaviour view associated with it – this relationship can be seen in Figure 4.3.

Each process behaviour view is realized in UML by an activity diagram that describes the behaviour of a single class or, in this context, a process. The activity diagram is made up of a number of elements, three of which are directly related to other parts of the meta-model:

- **The activity invocation**: represented by a sausage shape, this represents an activity from the process model, when using the terminology defined in Figure 4.5.

- **The object**: represented either by a box or by simple text, this represents an artefact.

- **The swim lane**: represented by two parallel lines and a label, this represents a role.

The activity diagram shows the order or execution of the activity invocations, together with any logical conditions associated with this order. It also shows the information flow, represented by the production and consumption of artefacts, around the flow of activity. Finally, the responsibility for each activity can be shown by using swim lanes that correspond to roles.

Figure 4.13 shows an example of a process behaviour view, in this case the one for the 'Meeting logistics' process shown in Figure 4.11. In this example, there are four swim lanes that represent the four responsible roles for this process. Each swim lane is responsible for the activities contained within it and the general flow of execution is shown by the order of execution of these activities.

The process behaviour view should be as simple as possible while still adding value to the process model. There are a few warning signs to look out for, however:

- A **single swim lane**: although this is certainly possible, it can often be an indication that the role identified is either the name of a person (rather than the stakeholder role name) who holds many roles, or that the role has been taken from too high in the hierarchy of the stakeholder view.

- **Too many possible execution paths**: remembering that complexity manifests itself through relationships rather than the nodes in the diagram, a diagram that is too messy or looks like a spider's web, should be avoided. In many cases this is the sign of a poorly understood or uncontrolled process. Bear in mind that some structure

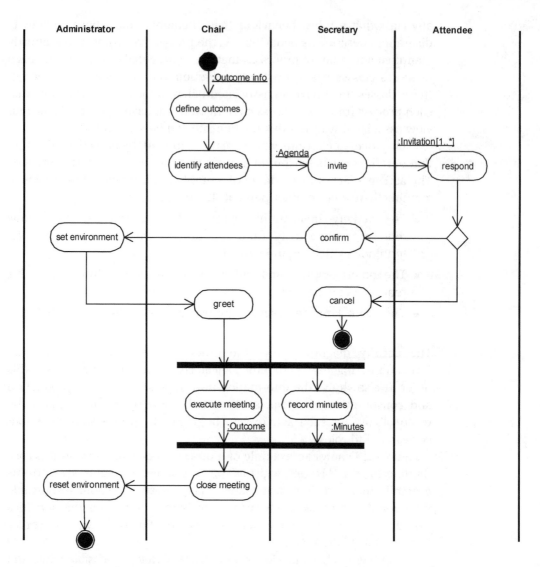

FIGURE 4.13 *Process behaviour view for the 'Meeting logistics' process*

should exist within the process, so having every activity invocation related to every other one is needless.

- **Single execution path**: some processes are truly linear in their behaviour with no possible deviation from the single thread of execution defined. Although this is possible, it is very unlikely in all but the most trivial of processes. Bear in mind that many processes will have at least one decision point involved – certainly any process that contains any sort of review, checking or testing activity will have at least two possible outcomes in each case. Where this is the case, there will be different paths of execution and iterations.

It is also possible to show any other roles that are involved, yet not responsible. This is done by showing participating roles in the activity invocation in brackets – for example '(Project manager)' – or may even be indicated by an actor (a stick person) with an association to the relevant activity invocation.

The information view

The information view is concerned with identifying the key artefacts from the system and then identifying their inter-relationships. This viewpoint is crucial for two main reasons:

- **Inter-process consistency**: a large part of the complexity involved with process models is derived from the interactions between the processes, rather than the internal working of each process. In order to make sure that processes are compatible (for example, that their respective inputs and outputs match up), it is vital to have an understanding of both the main artefacts of the processes and their inter-relationships.

- **Process automation**: if the process model is going to be used at a practical level by a group, or several groups, of people, then process automation is a point worth considering. In order to automate processes, it is important to understand what each artefact looks like (maybe a template will be defined for each one) and how these artefacts relate to one another. In fact, very often it is individual parts of each artefact that relate to other parts of artefacts, rather than the entire artefacts relating to one another.

The information view may be modelled at several levels of abstraction in order to represent the elements and their inter-relationships, and also the individual structure of each artefact.

The stakeholder view

The stakeholder view represents a simple classification of the different types of stakeholder roles that are involved with the process. The stakeholder view is realized in UML with a class diagram, with each stakeholder being represented by a single class.

It is typical for a single stakeholder view to be drawn up that represents many or, in some cases, all stakeholders in an organization, rather than creating one on a project-by-project basis. This is a tremendous help when it comes to trying to get an idea of the 'big picture' of an organization and can be invaluable when it comes to making sure that processes are consistent with one another.

The biggest mistake made by people when defining stakeholders is that they refer to stakeholders by individual names, such as the name of a person or an organization. It is the *role* of the person or organization, rather than the actual name that is of interest from the modelling point of view. There are several reasons for this:

- **Multiple roles**: it is possible and, indeed, very common for a single person to have more than one role. Consider the roles taken on by any single person in an organization and, in the vast majority of cases, each person will play more than one role. This is important as the roles played by an organization, for example, can be vastly different, yet have the same name associated with them.

- **Multiple names**: it is equally common for a single role to have many names associated with it. In some cases, particularly when it comes to users of a system, there can be millions of names associated with a single role.

- **Robustness**: by thinking of roles, rather than names, a model that is robust towards change is generated. Imagine how unmanageable the model would be if, every time that the name associated with a role changed, the model had to be changed. Not only is this impractical simply from people moving jobs (particularly in large organizations) but it is also possible that the number of names associated with a single role will increase as the project progresses through the development life cycle.

Therefore, always think of the role, rather than names when looking at stakeholders.

When generating a list of stakeholders, it is very easy to get things wrong for two totally different reasons. The first reason is that, invariably, if you were to write down a list of stakeholders associated with a process, there would be some missing. On the other hand, there will also be some stakeholders on the list who are not involved at all with the project. The only way to have any confidence that the stakeholder list is correct is to look at how and when the stakeholders occur on the different views of the process meta-model – a task that is straightforward, thanks to the diagram in Figure 4.3.

It is also difficult to know where to start thinking about stakeholders. Therefore, consider the very simple generic stakeholder view shown in Figure 4.14, which forces you to start thinking about the roles involved with a process or set of processes. Although this diagram will not be correct for many systems, it can serve as a good thought-provoker when initially considering a set of stakeholders.

There are three main types of 'Stakeholder' in Figure 4.14: 'Customer', 'External' and 'Supplier'. This three-way split is typical for many systems and can be a very good place to start thinking.

Three main 'Customer' stakeholder roles are identified here:

- 'User', which represents all the end users of a system. In the case of a transport system, this role would represent the passengers and, hence,

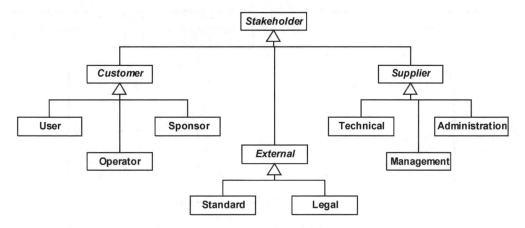

FIGURE 4.14 *Generic stakeholder view*

there may be millions of names associated with this role. Likewise, in a healthcare system, this role would represent the actual patients who are receiving treatment.

- 'Operator', which represents the people who will be configuring, controlling and operating the system. In the case of the transport system, this role would cover a range of roles from ticket sales, to driving the vehicles, to controlling the position of vehicles, route planning, and so on. In the case of the healthcare system, this role would again cover a number of other roles including doctors, nurses, surgeons, administrators, and so on.

- 'Sponsor', which represents whoever is providing the financial backing for the system. In the case of the transport system, this may be government related, private or some combination of the two. Similarly, the healthcare system may have a number of different names associated with it.

Two main 'External' roles are identified here:

- 'Standard', which represents standards and standards bodies that may constrain the development and operations of a system in some way. This may relate to safety standards, security, and so on.

- 'Legal', which relates to legal roles that may impact the system in some way, for example, data protection laws, health and safety legislation.

Three main 'Supplier' roles are identified here:

- 'Technical', which represents technical roles such as engineers, scientists and technicians.

- 'Management', which includes all management-related roles, such as project managers, risk managers and configuration managers.

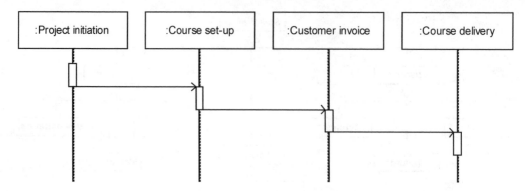

FIGURE 4.15 *Process instance view*

- 'Administration', which includes all administrative or support roles, such as secretaries, administrators, accountants and personnel staff.

There is also a natural link here to traditional organizational charts that, although not within the scope of this book, can form a valuable input for the stakeholders and a good source for validation of the roles that have been identified.

The process instance view

The process instance view comprises a set of diagrams that provides the main validation for the process model. It is the process instance view that relates the actual processes that are specified back to the source requirements and validates that each requirement has been met. The basic elements of the process instance view are executions of (or instances of) individual processes. For each requirement from the requirements view, it should be possible to execute a number of processes in a particular sequence in order to validate that requirement.

The process instance view is realized by a sequence diagram in the UML, with the main elements being executions of processes, represented in UML by life lines. Each life line represents a single, or group of, instances of a UML class or actor. Each life line has a dashed line below it that represents time, on which can be drawn one or more 'focus of control' that shows when the life line is active (i.e. doing something).

Figure 4.15 shows a simple sequence diagram. The life lines that go across the top of the diagram represent executions of individual instances of processes. The lines between show the flow of control between processes and can also be used to show any information flow of message passing.

This completes the discussion on the seven views of the process meta-model. The remainder of the chapter focuses on how to use the process meta-model effectively.

CONSISTENCY BETWEEN VIEWS

Consistency is the key to a good model – a model without consistency is simply a collection of drawings. It is impossible to have any degree of confidence in a process model that is inconsistent, as it is important that all the different views of the process model match with one another and, with the aid of the process meta-model, this is very straightforward. There are two main types of consistency checks to apply: structural checks and mechanical checks.

Structural checks may be applied based on the structure or pattern of the meta-model, particularly with respect to their relationships. Many of these checks can be identified based on the relationships in the meta-model.

Table 4.1 shows the specific structural consistency checks that should be applied that are based on the main associations in the process meta-model.

Mechanical checks involve selecting an element from the actual process model, identifying its corresponding class on the meta-model, and then looking for other occurrences of this class name on the meta-model. For example, consider the case where you need to apply consistency checks to stakeholders in the stakeholder view. First of all, look to the meta-model and find the class named 'Stakeholder' in the 'Stakeholder view'. The diagram indicates that the 'Stakeholder' in the 'Stakeholder view' is realized by a <<class>> in UML. Now, it is simply a matter of looking for other occurrences of stakeholder on the meta-model, which can be seen to be in the 'Process content view', where a 'Stakeholder' is realized by a <<Life line>>, and in the 'Requirements view', where a 'Stakeholder' is realized by an <<Actor>> in UML.

Table 4.1. *Structural consistency checks*

Check description	Meta-model reference
View check. Do all the views exist?	All classes that describe diagrams, for example: 'Information view' is realized by a <<class diagram>>
Process behaviour check. Does each process in the process content view have its behaviour defined?	'Process behaviour view' defines behaviour of each 'Process'
Is each requirement validated? Does each requirement have at least one scenario defined to ensure that the requirement is met?	'Process instance view' validates each 'Requirement'

Table 4.2. *Mechanical consistency checks*

Concept	View	Realized in UML by
Stakeholder	Requirements view	<<actor>>
	Process behaviour view	<<swim lane>>
	Stakeholder view	<<class>>
Activity	Process structure view	<<class>>
	Process content view	<<operation>>
	Process behaviour view	<<activity invocation>>
Artefact	Process structure view	<<class>>
	Process behaviour view	<<object>>
	Process content view	<<attribute>>
	Information view	<<class>>
Process	Process structure view	<<class>>
	Process content view	<<class>>
	Process instance view	<<life line>>

Table 4.2 shows the specific mechanical checks that should be applied, based on the common elements within the process meta-model. In order to use this table, select two views that need to be made consistent, for example those in Figures 4.11 and 4.13, which define the process content view and the process behaviour view for the 'Meeting logistics' process. In order to check the consistency of these two views, use Table 4.2 to look at the different elements of the diagram and how they relate to elements on its corresponding view. In this example, Figure 4.11, which is a class diagram, and Figure 4.13, which is an activity diagram, share the two terms 'Artefact' and 'Activity' from the meta-model. By looking these two terms up in Table 4.2 we can see that an 'Artefact' is an 'Object' in the process behaviour view and an 'Attribute' in the process content view. The same approach applies to the activity. By applying these simple mechanical checks, it becomes immediately apparent that the two views are actually inconsistent – something that needs to be remedied as soon as possible.

USING THE META-MODEL

Now that the meta-model has been defined, there are a number of ways that it can be used to add value to any process modelling exercise. This section introduces several different scenarios that explain how the process meta-model may be used and then discusses the advantages of its use for each scenario. This is not intended to be an exhaustive list of possible scenarios, but presents a good spread that illustrates the flexibility of the meta-model itself.

Analysing existing processes

In many cases, it is desirable to look at and analyse an existing process model. Some possible reasons for wanting to do this include:

- **As part of a process improvement exercise**: a process model is a living entity and, as such, it needs to be constantly monitored and, where necessary, changed and improved. This is such an important topic, that it has been given its own section heading.

- **To identify the causes of failure in the process**: it is relatively easy to simply define a process, but rather more difficult to ensure that it is an accurate reflection of real life and that it is effective. Therefore, these modelling techniques can be used to capture and analyse existing processes. This is particularly effective when trying to understand why something has gone wrong and can be a very powerful tool for examining the causes of failures and disasters. A key part of this is identifying which process has failed in some way, resulting in the system failure. Once the process causing the problem has been identified, it is then possible to look closer at the causes of the failure. It may be, for example, that the process itself is at fault and contains logical errors. A very common error is to miss off a feedback loop after a decision branch, such as after a review or similar activity. It may also be the case that the definition of the artefacts is inadequate and has led to the system failure. For example, perhaps not enough information has been recorded in an artefact or the wrong type of information has been recorded. Of course, another option is that the single process itself is not to blame, but that the process has not been executed properly or effectively, in which case the exercise could lead to the identification of another process, perhaps related to checking or monitoring that would prevent this type of failure recurring.

- **To gain an appreciation of an undocumented or complex process model**: in many cases, processes are represented as text descriptions, which can be very long and verbose. In such cases, it is desirable to have a simplified version of the process description so that an appreciation of how the process fits together and works can be gained. This is particularly powerful for looking at standards, processes and procedures that are out of the control of the actual organization, such as mandated standards and government initiatives.

- **As part of an audit or assessment**: when carrying out any sort of process-based audit or assessment, it is crucial to have an under-standing of both the process under review and the standard to which the process is being audited or assessed. This is actually a powerful combination of the first two points in this section – the standard being audited must be modelled to gain an appreciation and the standard being audited against must also be modelled. Of course, once these

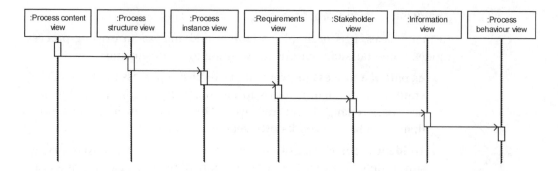

FIGURE 4.16 *Example scenario: Analysing existing processes*

source standards have been modelled once, they can be reused as often as desired and mapped onto other standards, which increases the added value of the modelling many times.

In terms of how the meta-model would be used for the previous points, Figure 4.16 shows an example scenario that represents the order of creation of the seven views when analysing an existing process model. The first view that is created is the process content view as, in cases where a process model exists and is well documented, this is often the easiest view to construct first. The process content view may then be used as a basis for abstracting the process structure view, as the structure can be most easily extracted from existing content. The next view to be created is the process instance view as, in many cases, examples of scenarios are given as part of the process description. From the process content view for the process model and the process instance view it is then possible to abstract right back up to the top-level requirements view. A natural progression from the requirements view and the process instance view is the stakeholder view, as many of the stakeholders will have been identified between each of these two views. The artefacts of the process model that have been identified from the process content view, and the information flow in the process instance view can now form the basis of the information view. Finally, the process behaviour views may be extracted from the low-level process descriptions.

Creating a new process document from scratch

In some cases, such as the start of a new business or perhaps the creation of a brand new process description for an impending audit or assessment, it is desirable to start a process description from scratch with, in effect, a blank sheet of paper. Although this situation does not occur very often in real-life industry, it is a very good exercise to get the feel for process modelling, whether it is to understand the how the modelling works or, indeed, to understand process models in the first place.

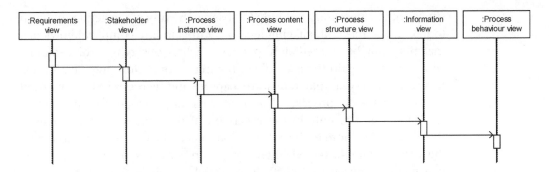

FIGURE 4.17 *Process instance view for creating a process model from scratch*

The generation of information in the situation of creating a process document from scratch can be summarized by creating a simple scenario, with the nodes on the diagram representing instances of the key views from the meta-model.

Figure 4.17 shows a sample scenario that represents creating a process document from scratch. As with all the situations, or scenarios, described in this section, the order of generation of the views is by no means carved in stone, but gives an idea of how the meta-model may be used in different ways.

In a situation like this, a good first step is to think about the requirements of the processes themselves. For example, the main requirement for a process may be to 'protect human life' in the case of a safety standard, or to 'process' applications in the case of a patient admission system. This highest-level requirement can then be broken down into lower-level requirements that can relate directly to processes. Also, it is usual for the highest-level requirements to have a number of constraints associated with them, for example meeting another standard, working in a particular environment or context, or even working with an existing system. It is also usual to start thinking about the stakeholders that interact with the processes at this point both by identifying actors in the requirements view and by generating an initial stakeholder view.

Once the requirements have been established, it is then possible to think about how these requirements could possibly be realized by identifying a number of scenarios. The key element of a scenario is that each node, or block, in the diagram represents the execution of a process. In this way, it is possible to create a list of processes that are needed together with the dependencies between them. Once the processes have been identified, there are a number of possible routes, such as defining the process content view, process structure view or even the information view.

Abstracting tacit process knowledge for a new system

It is often the case that the process knowledge required in order to create the process meta-model only exists inside people's heads. In such a situation, it is necessary not only to observe the process in action, but also to talk to the relevant stakeholders to try to gain any complex knowledge that may not be immediately perceived when observing. For example, consider once again the example of the magician performing a card trick. It is actually very simple to observe, capture and record the steps involved in the card-trick process. The problems arise when the process is replicated, as it is only in the execution of the process that you realize that there is far more to the process than meets the eye. It is easy to repeat the steps that are observed when a magician performs, but it is impossible to accurately reproduce the effects of a trick simply by following the steps involved. The whole art of magic is concerned with what is not perceived, deception, misdirection and downright lies! Although these are staple techniques employed deliberately by magicians, they are also techniques that are accidentally employed by many people when carrying out a process. An incomplete and inaccurate process description is often more harmful than no description at all.

It should be stressed here that there are many reasons why these techniques of deception are employed, such as:

- **Deliberate misdirection**: this often occurs in a working environment where the staff are unhappy – perhaps they don't take their job seriously, are worried about being replaced, or are simply mischievous. In such cases, it is important to know what questions to ask the relevant stakeholders and to compare the answers with other answers from the same stakeholder or maybe from other stakeholders. The process meta-model provides the information required to know which questions to ask which person at what time.

- **Misdirection by assumption**: assumption, as the old adage goes, is the mother of all foul-ups and the basic problem here is that the activities carried out by the stakeholder seem so obvious, that they are never mentioned. For example, when it comes to testing a TV set, before any tests can be carried out the TV set must have the power switched on. It is this type of obvious information that is often omitted as people simply *assume* that it is known or done.

- **Misdirection by ignorance**: it may be that the stakeholder who is describing the process does not fully understand the process in the first place. In such situations, it is unlikely that an accurate process description will be provided.

Figure 4.18 shows the order in which the seven views are created to deal with this situation. The first view that is generated is the stakeholder view, as this identifies which roles exist and provides a basis for knowing who to talk to concerning the process behaviours. Therefore, the second view to be generated is the process behaviour view, which consists of a number of diagrams – one for each process with activities. Once the process behaviours have been created, it is then possible to abstract the process

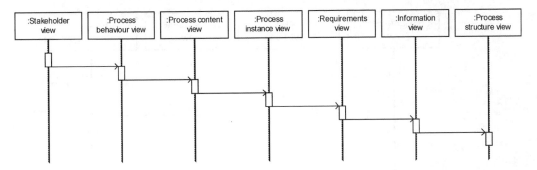

FIGURE 4.18 *Process instance for abstracting tacit process knowledge for a new system*

content view from them and, from there, the process instance view. From the process instance view and the process content view, it is then possible to create the requirements view and the information view. Finally, the process structure view is abstracted.

Abstracting tacit process knowledge for an existing system

This situation is similar to the previous one except, in this case, there is some recorded process information already in existence. Therefore, the class of 'Process knowledge' from Figure 4.1 may be realized by written information, standards and existing process models.

Figure 4.19 shows the order of creation of the seven views for the situation for abstracting tacit process knowledge for an existing system. In this case, the process structure view is created first, based on the limited process knowledge available. It is then possible to generate the process content view and, from this, the information view. The stakeholder view is generated next which, again, is abstracted from existing documentation. Now that the stakeholders and the processes have been identified, it is possible to put them together into scenarios and to generate the process instance view. As the process instance view and the process content view

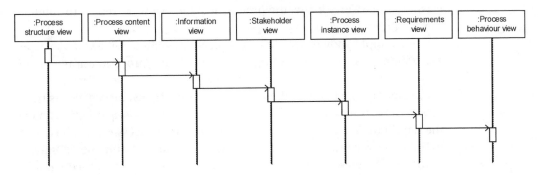

FIGURE 4.19 *Process instance for abstracting tacit process knowledge for an existing system*

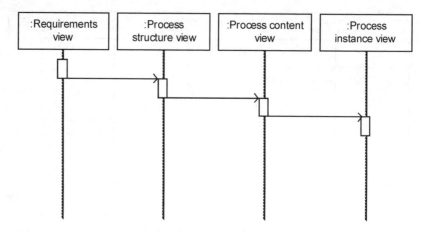

FIGURE 4.20 *Process instance for process improvement*

have been identified, the requirements view can be abstracted. Finally, the detailed process behaviour view may be generated.

Process improvement for existing processes

This situation occurs when there is an existing process model that has been well defined and well documented. As part of the continuous process improvement exercise, a basic review is carried out every six months and, rather than a full process model analysis as shown in Figure 4.16, this time a partial analysis is carried out.

Figure 4.20 shows the situation for process improvement. The first view that is generated here is the requirements view. This is done to check that the original requirements for the process model have not changed in any way. Once the requirements have been checked and any new requirements added, the process structure view is generated to check that the basic framework of the process model is unchanged. The main part of this exercise is then to look at the process content view to identify all the existing processes. Finally, the process instance view is created to validate the requirements view.

The example shown here does not need to include all seven views, as everything has gone according to plan in the process improvement exercise – there are no changes to be made.

Consider now what would happen if the process instance view has been used as a basis for a gap analysis to ensure that the existing processes meet the requirements. Where gaps are found, the new processes must be added to the process content view. This would then entail creating the remainder of the seven views, as there has been a major change to the process model and, hence, all views must be revisited.

General notes

It should be stressed that the examples discussed here are just that – examples. Do not feel constrained by the scenarios provided here, as each one could be changed; there just needs to be some rationale behind the order that is specified in the process instance.

In terms of the order of creation of the views, it should be clear by now that there is no strict order that is carved in stone, as the actual order will depend on the situation at hand. There are, however, a few common patterns in the various process instance views shown here, which is only natural, as they are based on the structural consistency checks described in Table 4.1. The structural checks are based on the associations in the process meta-model, therefore, if the process content view and the requirements view are known, then the process instance view is an obvious place to go next. Likewise, if the process instance view and the stakeholder view are known, the requirements view might be a good next move.

Keep in mind that the more that the process meta-model is understood and becomes ingrained as a natural part of process modelling, then the more natural these scenarios will become, and the more robust the final process models will be.

EXTENDING THE PROCESS META-MODEL

The process meta-model is a very powerful tool, but its application does not stop at process analysis, definition, mapping and visualization; it may be extended to include a number of process-related applications. As an example of the flexibility of the process meta-model and its potential use in an organization, consider a very important issue, that of project schedules.

Process modelling for life cycle management

Any project requires an element of project planning and the generation of some sort of project schedule. A project schedule is usually realized in some sort of Gantt chart or Pert chart which are, themselves, a form of visual modelling. However, such schedules are often wildly inaccurate when it comes to representing the actual activities that are carried out by the workers involved with the project and are often regarded as a work of fiction by the people doing the work. Consider the horrific examples concerning project overruns in the field of, for example, IT systems. It is possible to pick up any newspaper in any given week of the year and find examples of projects that have been absolute disasters. For detailed examples of these see (Flowers, 1996).

Such cost and time overruns are quite common but, in many cases, this is not necessarily a fault of the people carrying out the work but more a case of the project not meeting the initial expectations of the project

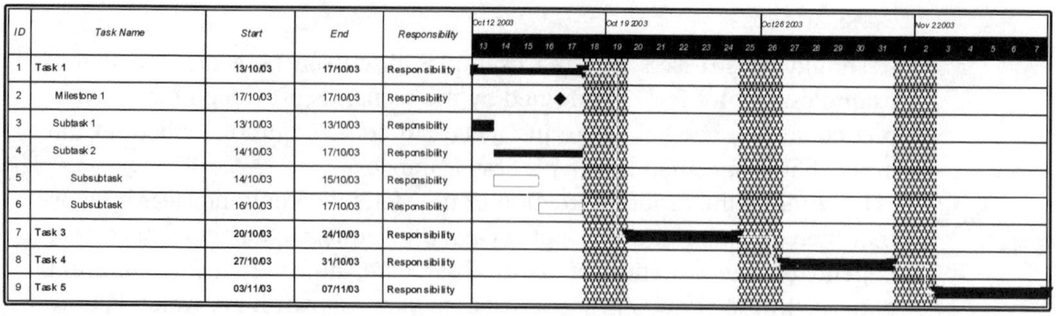

ID	Task Name	Start	End	Responsibility	Oct 12 2003					Oct 19 2003							Oct 26 2003						Nov 22 2003						
					13	14	15	16	17	18	19	20	21	22	23	24	25	26	27	28	29	30	31	1	2	3	4	5	6	7
1	Task 1	13/10/03	17/10/03	Responsibility																											
2	Milestone 1	17/10/03	17/10/03	Responsibility																											
3	Subtask 1	13/10/03	13/10/03	Responsibility																											
4	Subtask 2	14/10/03	17/10/03	Responsibility																											
5	Subsubtask	14/10/03	15/10/03	Responsibility																											
6	Subsubtask	16/10/03	17/10/03	Responsibility																											
7	Task 3	20/10/03	24/10/03	Responsibility																											
8	Task 4	27/10/03	31/10/03	Responsibility																											
9	Task 5	03/11/03	07/11/03	Responsibility																											

FIGURE 4.21 *Typical generic Gantt chart*

schedule. One indicator of the expectations of the project can be found in the project schedule which, if very unrealistic, will by its very nature result in time and hence cost overruns. Therefore, where does the fault lie – with the people carrying out the work to the best of their ability, or in the unrealistic expectations of the project managers who set unrealizable goals?

These inaccurate estimates of times, costs and resources are inexcusable, and mostly avoidable, when a full knowledge of the processes in an organization are known. On one level, all that a Gantt chart represents is the execution of processes during the course of a project. If these processes are well defined and have been carried out before, then there is no reason why realistic estimates cannot be put on the process activities at the lowest level, such as in the process behavioural view, and then aggregated up into realistic timing estimations. Of course, in real life there will be timing constraints imposed on a project from day 1, but it is possible to provide an accurate estimation of the time required to execute the relevant processes and then see if they meet the original project constraints.

As an example of this, consider a typical Gantt chart, such as the one in Figure 4.21, where the project tasks are broken down into three levels of detail:

- the major task level, represented by the thick black line that shows the highest grouping of project activity;
- the subtask level, which is a decomposition of the task level and shows a more detailed view of what project activity is occurring;
- the subsubtask level, which is a decomposition of the subtask level and shows a more detailed view of what project activity is occurring.

Also, other information, such as key milestones, dates and resources, may be indicated on the chart. All of this information can be derived directly from the process meta-model and, if this application is to be used extensively, it is possible to extend the process meta-model to include project management information, as shown in Figures 4.22 and 4.23.

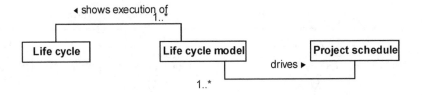

FIGURE 4.22 *Process concept view for the schedule enhancement*

Remembering that the original meta-model contains a conceptual and realization aspect, then Figures 4.22 and 4.23 should be viewed as extensions to the existing meta-model.

Figure 4.22 shows the additional information required to make the process meta-model concept view usable for project scheduling purposes. In this case, project management concepts are captured in the form of a class diagram. Of course, this extension will differ depending on the approach taken to project management within the organization. Like all the information in the meta-model, this must be tailored, but the tailoring here has the potential to be far more significant than the changes required for the standard meta-model, simply due to the numbers of different approaches that are possible for project management.

Figure 4.22 shows the enhancement to the process concept view for the process meta-model. The new concepts that have been introduced here are:

- 'Life cycle', which identifies the phases in the project, but does not imply any sort of order.

- 'Life cycle model', which defines how the phases in the life cycle are executed. The life cycle is a structural view, whereas the life cycle model is a behavioural view.

- 'Project schedule', which defines how the overall project will be executed and includes time, cost and resource information.

The key point shown on the diagram is the set of associations between the new concepts, as this will form the basis for mapping onto the existing process meta-model. The relationships between these new concepts and the existing process meta-model can now be explored by looking at these concepts in more detail and also by defining how each concept will be realized using modelling.

Once these concepts have been captured, their realization must be defined in order to make the meta-model usable.

Figure 4.23 shows the process meta-model realization view for the project management extension to the meta-model. In this case, the target visualization for the schedule information is not UML but the Gantt chart. Therefore, the stereotypes that indicate how the concepts are realized

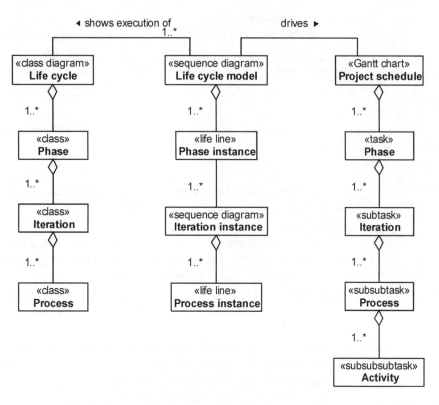

FIGURE 4.23 *Possible extension to the process meta-model*

relate to Gantt chart terminology, rather than UML terminology. Of course, there is no reason why this realization should be limited to Gantt charts as, providing that the language and notation is understood, then any form of visualization, such as Pert charts or even a proprietary notation may be adopted.

This process realization view may now be mapped onto the existing one to provide an extended process meta-model. The way that the two views are related will be in terms of relating the main concepts and then by identifying common concepts. For example, a relationship will be added, such as, 'Life cycle' uses the 'Process model'. This forms the main link back to the original process model. The next mapping can be achieved by looking at common terms used between the old view and the new view. Therefore, the following relationships will exist:

- 'Process', which exists as part of an iteration and is represented by a <<class>>, is the same as the concept of a 'Process' in Figure 4.3.

- 'Process instance', which exists as part of an iteration instance and is represented by a <<life line>>, is the same as the concept of a 'Process instance' in Figure 4.3.

- 'Process', which exists as an iteration, again, but is represented by a <<subsubtask>> (part of the Gantt chart terminology), is the same as the concept of the 'Process' in Figure 4.3.

These basic mappings will also form consistency checks that apply to the extended meta-model.

The extension to the meta-model shown here is simply an example and, as with all aspects of process modelling, must be tailored for a particular situation and organization. The intention here is to show the potential for the use of the meta-model, but this need not be limited to project schedules – consider the following applications that may be catered for by an extended process meta-model:

- **Capability determination**: what capabilities can a company offer as part of their service or product to customers? By looking at the processes that the organization can offer, it is possible to abstract a number of capabilities that can then be 'sold' to potential clients. Capabilities and processes should not be confused, as the process represents the core activities, whereas the capability reflects more the application.

- **Tender application**: evaluating and applying for tenders should be based on the capabilities that the organization can offer and, hence, the processes. If a request for proposals can be represented as a requirements view, then the processes in the organization can be mapped onto these requirements to demonstrate that the project requirements can be met. Of course, this will also identify any gaps in the existing process model that need to be filled before the work can carried out.

- **Skillset identification for recruitment**: each stakeholder represents a role that will have a number of required skills and, if this is built into the meta-model, it can then be used as a basis for recruitment activities. This will be touched upon in the case study in Chapter 6.

The point here is to try not to be limited in using the meta-model, but to look at other areas in which it may be used. After all, processes are fundamental to everything that we do, therefore, the meta-model has many applications.

CONCLUSIONS

This chapter discussed the process meta-model in more detail, in terms of the concepts and how they are realized. This realization takes the form of the seven views that comprise the process meta-model. In order to fully specify a process, all seven views are essential. Each of these views is realized using the UML and a number of consistency checks have been defined based on the structure of the meta-model. Although the description of the meta-model formed the main part of the chapter, the application of the meta-model will provide the tangible benefits to businesses. Therefore, several scenarios were described detailing different applications of the meta-model. Finally, the chapter demonstrated how the meta-model can be extended for different applications, in particular, here, project schedules.

The meta-model should be tailored for particular organizations, as terms and practices will differ, but the pattern of the meta-model will, in most cases, remain very similar.

5 Process Mapping and Metrics

'I'm no good at judging the size of crowds, Ted, but I'd say there's about seventeen million of them out there'

Father Dougal McGuire, *Father Ted*, Channel 4

INTRODUCTION

The benefits of having a well-defined process are many, and one of these is to give people confidence in the way that you do things. For example, a customer may want some degree of confidence in a capability offered by your organization. There are several ways to demonstrate this confidence, and one of these is to demonstrate that the approach adopted is a valid and accepted one.

The way that an approach is demonstrated is usually carried out in one of two ways: through an assessment or through an audit. The process model that is being audited or assessed against (usually a standard) is referred to as the *source process*, whereas the process model under review is referred to as the *target process*. In both audits and assessments, there are three aspects of the process model that are being examined:

- **Source standard compliance**: whether or not there is a basic mapping between the source standard and the target process.

- **Process implementation**: whether or not the target process is being implemented on real projects. Examples of the use of processes being used on projects or process instances, as they are known, are sought and then these are either audited or assessed.

- **Process effectiveness**: whether or not the process is effective. Are any metrics being taken and is the process then being improved as time goes on? Are the requirements for the process correct and up to date?

Although both assessments and audits share the same basic aims, they are executed in very different ways:

- **Audit**: an audit tends to be more formal than an assessment. An audit is usually carried out by a third-party, an independent body, to enforce the source standard. This source standard, for example ISO 9001 (2000), must be well understood and the audit will often make use of specific 'checklists' that enable each part of the standard to be checked against the target process. For an audit, a documented process model must exist, otherwise the full audit cannot take place.

The output of an audit is typically a straight 'pass' or 'fail' result with an indication of which specific parts of the source process were not met – or 'non-compliances' as they are often known.

- **Assessment**: an assessment tends to be more informal than an audit and may be carried out either by independent third-parties or by suitably-qualified people inside the organization. Examples of assessment standards include ISO 15504 (ISO/IEC, 2004) and CMMI (Carnegie Mellon Software Engineering Institute, 2002). An assessment starts out with a blank sheet of paper, the target process is then abstracted and the results of this abstraction are then assessed. This means that the target process may be well documented, in which case the abstraction is relatively simple, or there may be no documentation whatsoever (the process exists purely in someone's head) in which case the abstraction is not so straightforward. Of course, one advantage of this is that *any* target process may be effectively assessed, even if it is not formally documented. The output of an assessment is typically a profile, rather than a simple 'pass' or 'fail', that provides effective feedback about how mature each process is. There is usually a scale of five or so levels that indicates the maturity – a low number indicating an immature and uncontrolled process and a high number indicating a mature and controlled process.

A common aspect of both approaches is being able to demonstrate basic compliance between the source standard and the target process, and this is where, initially, process mapping comes in.

There are several inherent problems associated with process mapping:

- **Terminology differences**: perhaps the most common problem between different standards or process models is one of communication – the actual terminology is very different. For example, consider the different words that may be employed to indicate the activities (using the terminology adopted in this book) within a process – words such as: 'task', 'step', 'practice', 'action'. Although these seem like minor differences, what about the situation where the same word is used, such as 'process', but with different definitions in each process. It is essential, therefore, that these differences in language can be identified and clarified.

- **Volume of data**: in many cases, it is desirable to map, not just between two processes, but between many. It is not uncommon to find a list of relevant standards, either in a requirements specification or in a project contract that forms a formal obligation for the project. Bear in mind, however, that realistically if there are 50 standards listed, this means, potentially, 50 audits or assessments must be carried out. The sheer volume of data involved here, not to mention the time and effort involved, would be phenomenal.

- **Meaningful metrics**: there is an old adage that anything that can't be measured, can't be controlled, therefore it is important that measurements and, hence, metrics can be applied to the process mapping in order to demonstrate how effective the mapping is. However, coming up with meaningful metrics is often difficult, so any effective process mapping should be capable of being measured in some way.

The remainder of this chapter defines an example of a process for process mapping that meets all of the requirements laid out above. Of course, this process is merely an example and is not the only approach that can be taken to perform process mapping, but it is one that has proven to be simple yet effective for real-life situations.

A PROCESS FOR PROCESS MAPPING

This section describes a process for process mapping. Of course, this process is described in UML, so it is an excellent example of how the modelling can be used to specify a process. The process is expressed in terms of the process meta-model and each of the views is presented here.

As each view is presented, the complexity of each diagram will also be discussed, together with any consistency checks that are applied between the various views. One point to bear in mind here is that complexity can occur on any view, which is why it is so important to look at all the views from the process meta-model.

The process structure view

The process structure view is the same as the one already defined (see Chapter 4) and will not be replicated here. This uses all the same terminology as has been used throughout this book.

The requirements view

The first view that we will consider is the requirements view, which explains why we are defining the process mapping process in the first place. This is realized in the use case diagram in Figure 5.1.

Figure 5.1 shows a simple requirements view for a mapping process. At the moment, this is modelled at a high level of abstraction and will be described in more detail later in this section. Note that the main requirement is stated quite simply as 'develop process mapping process', which has three actors associated with it: the 'Process engineer', which represents the person or group of people who will be developing the process; the 'Source process', which represents the model to be mapped against; and, finally, the 'Reviewer'. There is one single constraint on this requirement, which is to 'inspire confidence' and is related to the 'Sponsor' and the 'Standard enforcer'. In this case, the exercise is being

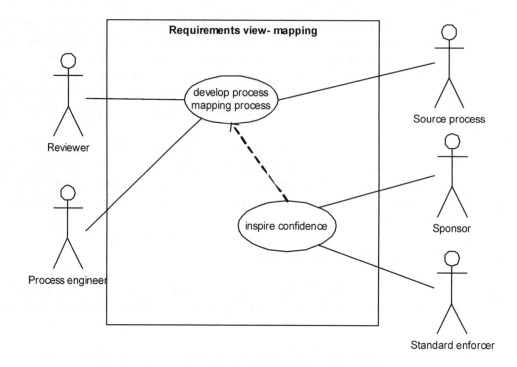

FIGURE 5.1 *Simple requirements view*

carried out at the request of sponsors, who require some confidence that their processes map onto the relevant standards. The standards enforcer is involved as any mapping that is produced and any compliance issues will need to be approved by the appropriate authority.

The stakeholder view

The stakeholder view can be abstracted from the actors that were identified in the requirements view, and then arranged into a classification hierarchy.

Figure 5.2 identifies the stakeholder roles that are relevant to the project. These stakeholders are consistent with the actors on the stakeholder view and also the names that govern each swim lane in the process behaviour view. The roles that have been identified are as follows:

- 'Sponsor': the person or organization who is paying for the process mapping exercise, maybe as part of an audit or assessment.
- 'Standard enforcer': the people who will be carrying out the audit or assessment. In the case of an audit, these people are independent of the target organization or, in the case of an assessment, they may be either internal or external to the target organization.

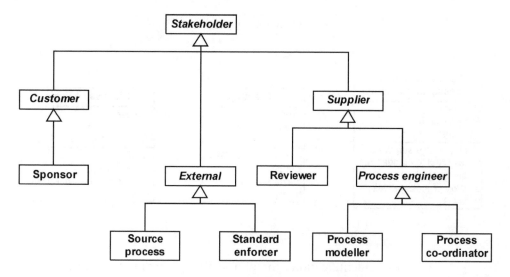

FIGURE 5.2 *Stakeholder view*

- 'Process engineer': the person or people who are defining the process mapping approach. In this case, there are two roles defined as types of 'Process engineer' which are the 'Process modeller', who performs all modelling activities and the 'Process co-ordinator' who manages and controls the exercise.

- 'Source process': this role represents the source standard. It may seem a little odd to have a process model as a stakeholder, but it meets all the requirements of being one – it is outside the boundary of the system and has an interest in the project.

Now that the requirements and the stakeholders have been identified, it is time to look at the actual processes that need to be defined in order to meet these requirements.

The process content view

The process content view, for the process mapping application, consists initially of three processes as shown in Figure 5.3.

Figure 5.3 shows the process content view that identifies the processes that have been created along with their relevant artefacts (represented by attributes) and activities (represented by operations). In this case, three processes have been identified as being necessary to meet the requirements shown in Figure 5.1. All of these processes could have been shown as a single process, but consider the number of attributes and operations for that single class and imagine how the complexity would increase.

The three processes that have been identified are described as follows:

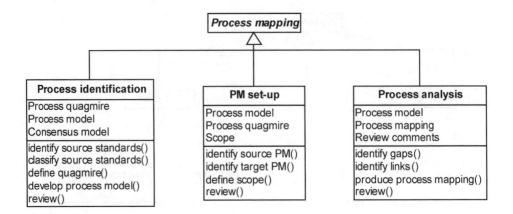

FIGURE 5.3 *Process content view*

- 'Process identification': the aim of this process is to identify all the relevant source processes that are applicable to the mapping exercise. One of the main outputs here is the 'Process quagmire', which is a variation of the information view and is realized by a class diagram where each class represents a different source process. In the situation where only a single source standard is being used, this quagmire is quite simple (more of a puddle than a quagmire), however, as soon as more than one source process is used, the complexity increases and the quagmire becomes deeper and deeper.

- 'PM set-up': the main aim of this process is to define the scope of the assessment or audit (which processes in the target process will be evaluated) and then to identify the relevant parts of each source process.

- 'Process analysis': the aim of this process is to actually perform the mapping between the source processes and the target process. This involves looking for links between them as well as gaps.

In terms of the way that these processes are executed, they are quite 'tightly coupled'. This means that the relationships between the processes are actually dependencies and, hence, does not allow for much freedom in terms of variation of execution. This can be seen more clearly in the slightly extended diagram in Figure 5.4.

Figure 5.4 shows dependencies between the three processes, which highlights the high degree of coupling between them. In reality, this translates as restricting the order of execution of the processes. This can be illustrated by looking at the process instance view.

The process instance view

The processes that were identified in the process content view can now be executed in order to meet the original requirements. Bearing in mind that

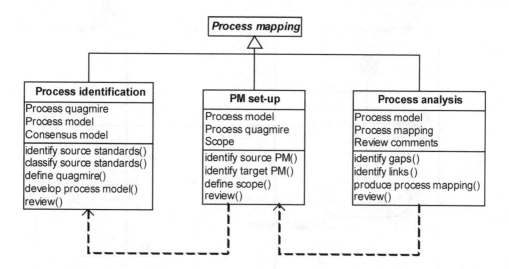

FIGURE 5.4 *Extended process content view*

there were dependencies identified between these processes, this constrains the number of different scenarios that can be applied.

Figure 5.5 shows a single scenario for executing the processes defined in the process content view. In this case, this is because of the limitations imposed by the dependencies defined in Figure 5.4. The order of execution for the processes has been defined, but not the execution of each individual process, which will be defined in the process behaviour view.

The process behaviour view

A process behaviour view is defined for each of the processes defined in Figure 5.3.

Figure 5.6 shows *how* the 'Process identification' process behaves over time. Each of the activity invocations (represented by the sausage shapes) is checked for consistency against the operations from the parent class. The information flow is represented by simple text statements that are

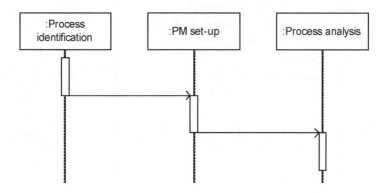

FIGURE 5.5 *Process instance view for the mapping exercise*

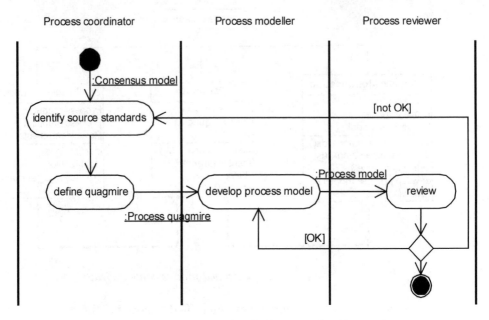

FIGURE 5.6 *Process behaviour view for the 'Process identification' process*

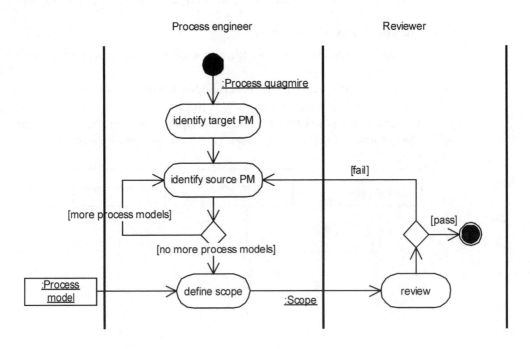

FIGURE 5.7 *Process behaviour view for the 'PM set-up' process*

associated with the flows between the activity invocations. This information is a set of instances of the attributes from the parent class. The final
piece of information that is specified here is the responsibility for each
activity invocation that is grouped by using swim lanes (represented by the
parallel vertical lines). Any activity invocation that lies within the
boundaries of a swim lane is defined as being the responsibility of the
stakeholder role that is specified at the top of each swim lane.

Figure 5.7 shows the process behaviour view for the 'PM set-up' process.
Note the two representations of UML objects being used here to represent
the process artefacts. The short form is to use simple text and a colon, as in
':Process quagmire' which works well when there is a sequential
information flow throughout the process. However, in some situations,
information is coming in from outside the process part-way through its
execution. In such cases, it is more usual to see the artefact represented in
a rectangle, as in 'Process model'.

Figure 5.8 shows the process behaviour view for the 'Process analysis'
process. Note the use of UML control splits and joins here to show that
there is no specific order to the execution of the activities 'identify gaps'
and 'identify links'. Although the concurrent operation shown here is

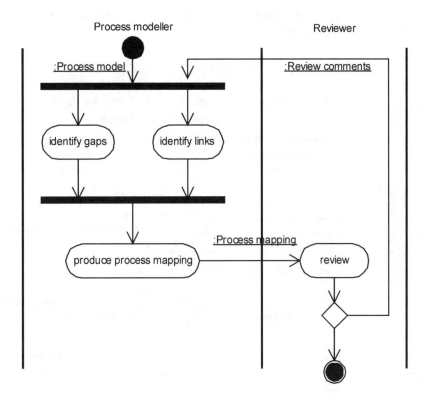

FIGURE 5.8 *Process behaviour view for the 'Process analysis' process*

101

meaningful, it is very easy to fall into the trap of making all activities concurrent, which results in a flat structure in the pattern of the model. When such flat structures occur, it is usually a sign of a poorly thought-out process behaviour and can often lead to management problems when the process is executed, as there is no semblance of order to the activity invocations.

The information view

The information view for the process mapping processes relates all the artefacts together, and can be seen in Figure 5.9. From the diagram, it can be seen that there is a 'Consensus model' representing a set of requirements that provides the background information needed for all the process models (the 'Process model' class) to be identified. There are two types of 'Process model': the single 'Target process' and the one or more 'Source process'. A 'Process quagmire' is produced that identifies the relationships between all the process models that have been identified. The 'Scope' defines a subset of the 'Target process' identifying a subset of processes in the target process that will form the basis of the assessment. The mapping between the source standards and the single target process is captured in the 'Process mapping', and this is commented upon and the results captured in the 'Review comments'.

This completes the process description for the process mapping processes.

PROCESS MAPPING METRICS

So far, the processes that have been defined have been concerned with the actual process mapping itself and do not include any form of measurement nor the application of metrics.

Metrics can take many shapes and sizes, and it is important to have a process defined for their application. The process that will be defined here

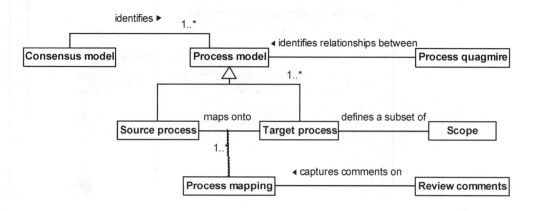

FIGURE 5.9 *Information view for process mapping*

is concerned with calculating the number of mappings (relationships) between two process models and involves some very simple measurements (mainly counting), and calculating some simple metrics based on these measurements.

In order to define the metrics process, the process model defined so far must have a number of its views extended, in particular: the process content view, the process behaviour view and the information view.

The extended process content view

The process content view is extended by introducing a new process. Figure 5.10 shows the new process, 'Metric application', that must be added to the process content view. Note the interesting use of multiplicity here on the attributes of the class. Although this is by no means compulsory, it is often useful to show that an attribute will manifest itself more than once. In this case, several of the attributes have a multiplicity of one-to-many, indicated as [1..*].

The extended information view

The key to the metrics application process lies in the extension to the information view, as the process itself is very much dependent on the measurements that are being taken. These measurements and subsequent metrics are defined more clearly in the information view.

Figure 5.11 shows the extended information view that relates the measurements and metrics to the process structure view. Note that only a

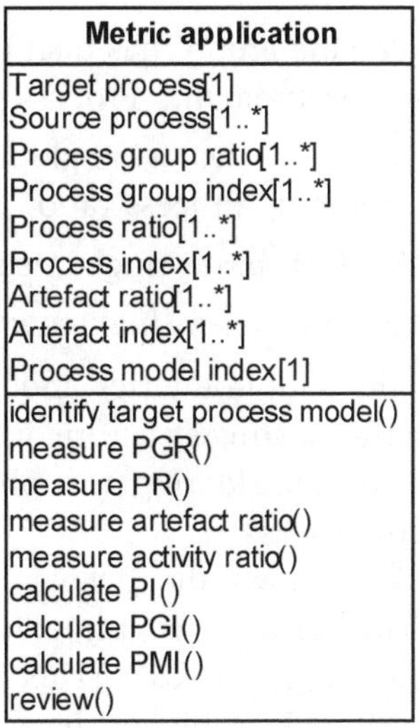

Metric application
Target process[1]
Source process[1..*]
Process group ratio[1..*]
Process group index[1..*]
Process ratio[1..*]
Process index[1..*]
Artefact ratio[1..*]
Artefact index[1..*]
Process model index[1]
identify target process model()
measure PGR()
measure PR()
measure artefact ratio()
measure activity ratio()
calculate PI()
calculate PGI()
calculate PMI()
review()

FIGURE 5.10 *New process for the process content view*

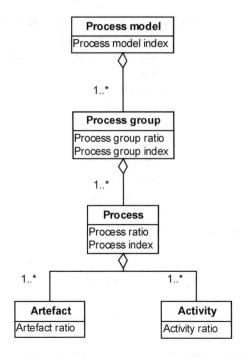

FIGURE 5.11 *Extended information view*

subset of the process structure view is shown here – just the parts that have measurements or metrics applied to them. Therefore, it can be seen from Figure 5.11 that:

- The 'Process model' has a single metric, identified as the 'Process model index'.
- The 'Process group' has a single metric, 'Process group index' and a single measurement, 'Process group ratio'.
- The 'Process' has a single metric, 'Process index' and a single measurement, 'Process ratio'.
- The 'Artefact' has a single measurement, 'Artefact ratio'.
- The 'Activity' has a single measurement, 'Activity ratio'.

Now that the simple metrics and measurements have been defined and applied to the existing structure, it is time to look at how they are actually generated, by considering the process behaviour view for the 'Metric application' process.

Figure 5.12 shows the behavioural view for the 'Metric application' process. This process is immediately more complex than any of the process mapping processes. There is far more iteration in this process, which results in a higher level of complexity and the amount of information is also far higher.

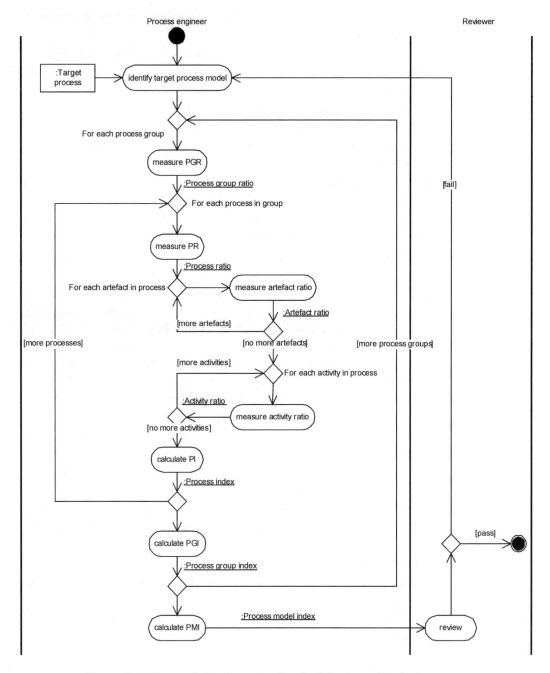

FIGURE 5.12 *Process behaviour view for the 'Metric application' process*

Each of the activities in the process must be described in more detail. This can be done using more activity diagrams or using text descriptions. At some point in the process modelling exercise, each element will have a text description associated with it. The activity descriptions are as follows:

- 'identify target process model': this activity just confirms the inputs to the process.

- 'measure PGR': the PGR, or process group ratio, is the ratio between the number of process groups (or equivalent terms) for both standards.

- 'measure PR': for each process group, there will be a certain number of processes contained therein. The PR, or process ratio, is the ratio between the number of processes in each process group. Therefore, there will be a PR measurement for each process group.

- 'measure artefact ratio': for each process, there will be a number of artefacts and the artefact ratio is the ratio between each artefact in the target process and the source process. Therefore, there will be an artefact ratio for each artefact in the process.

- 'measure activity ratio': similar to the artefact ratio, but this time based on the number of activities, rather than artefacts.

- 'calculate PI': the PI, or process index, provides a measure of mapping between the processes. The process index is calculated by counting the number of artefacts and activities that have a non-zero ratio (for example, 2:0, is a zero ratio, whereas 4:3 is a non-zero ratio) for their artefact and activity ratios and then dividing this by the total number of artefacts and activities. Therefore, a process that has artefacts and activities that map completely to the source process has a PI of 1, whereas any incomplete ratios result in a PI of less than 1.

- 'calculate PGI': the PGI, or process group index, is calculated by adding each PI for the processes in the process group and dividing by the number of processes in that group. Again, a complete mapping will result in a PGI of 1.

- 'calculate PMI': the PMI, or process model index, is calculated by adding each PGI for the process group in the process model and then dividing by the total number of process groups. Again, a complete process mapping will result in a PMI of 1.

- 'review': a review of the artefacts and the content of each artefact for this process.

These descriptions are used in the next section when the process is implemented.

APPLICATION OF METRICS

The processes associated with process mapping and metrics have been defined, but these processes have not yet been executed. This section, therefore, is concerned with applying these processes.

The processes defined in this chapter are applied in the order defined in the process instance view in Figure 5.5, that is:

1. process identification;
2. PM set-up;
3. process analysis.

The 'Process identification' process

The 'identify source standards' activity

The source standards will be: ISO/IEC 15504, *Software Process Assessment* (2004), ISO 15288, *Systems engineering: Systems life cycle processes* (2002), ISO 9001, *Model for quality assurance in design, development, production, installation and servicing* (2000), ISO 12207, *Information technology: Software life cycle processes* (2004) and CMMI (Carnegie Mellon Software Engineering Institute, 2002). These were chosen based on the 'Consensus' model, which is simply a statement of requirements for the exercise. In some cases this will be recorded in a specification report, while in other cases it may be abstracted from talking to people, conducting interviews, surveys, and so on.

The 'define quagmire' activity

The quagmire identifies any related standards or processes that may have an influence on the process mapping exercise. Figure 5.13 shows a process quagmire for the exercise, where 'ISO 15288' is related to 'ISO 12207', which is related to 'ISO 9001'. Also, 'ISO 15288' is related to 'ISO 15504' which is related to 'CMM'.

This diagram is still relatively simple, but for an excellent example of how complex such diagrams can be, see The Frameworks Quagmire at www.software.org/quagmire.

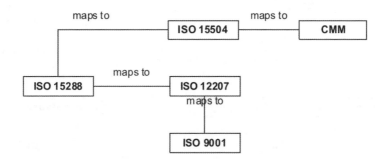

FIGURE 5.13 *Process quagmire*

If this exercise was taken further, it would be possible to provide a full mapping between all of these standards based on the relationships between them in the quagmire.

The 'develop process model' activity

In this activity, any necessary process models will be produced. The two main views that will be used as a basis for the basic process mapping are the process structure view and the process content view.

Figure 5.14 shows the process structure view for both the source and target processes. On the left is the structure of ISO 15288, which is the target process, and on the right is ISO 15504, which is the source process. There is an immediate similarity between the two structures, in fact the pattern is identical. Note, however, the difference in terminology that is being used here. Therefore, there is an immediate benefit from putting these two views side-by-side as straightaway a mapping between terms has been established.

The next level down in the process structure view looks at the grouping level for each standard.

Figure 5.15 shows a lower-level aspect of the process structure view for both standards, but this time the emphasis is on the grouping level. By looking at these two views side-by-side, the patterns are not immediately obvious, but, upon closer inspection, it will be demonstrated that there is indeed a mapping between them.

When looking for where a mapping exists between two process models, it is important to look at the different levels of abstraction in the models. For example, in Figure 5.15 it is tempting to map at the highest levels ('Process group' to 'Process category') and then to drop down to the next

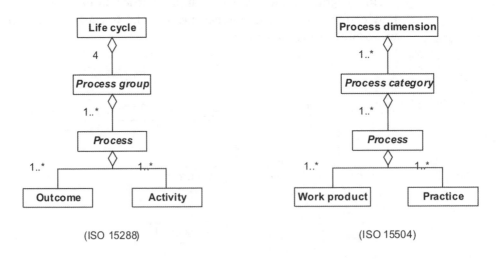

(ISO 15288)   (ISO 15504)

FIGURE 5.14 *Process structure views for ISO 15288 and 15504*

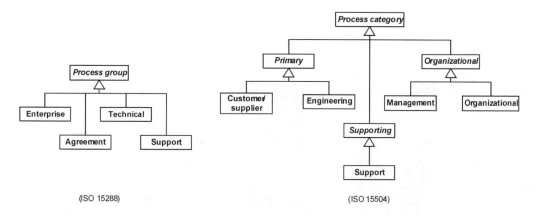

(ISO 15288)   (ISO 15504)

FIGURE 5.15 *Process structure views, with an emphasis on the grouping level, for the standards*

level and map across. This would result in a second-level mapping of 'Enterprise', 'Agreement', 'Technical' and 'Support' directly to 'Primary', 'Supporting' and 'Organizational'. This would leave the third level for ISO 15504 with no mapping. In this situation, this is incorrect, as the second level of the ISO 15504 process model ('Primary', 'Supporting' and 'Organizational') is simply another level of classification, and the correct mapping is between 'Enterprise', 'Agreement', 'Technical' and 'Support' in ISO 15288, and 'Customer/supplier', 'Engineering', Support', 'Management' and 'Organizational' in ISO 15504.

Therefore, it is important to think about each mapping rather than just assuming that all levels will map exactly.

Figure 5.16 shows the process content view for both standards. This is not the entire process content view but is the subset of the target process model that will defined by the scope. Again, the basic patterns look quite different, but this will be explored during the 'Process analysis' process.

The 'review' activity

At this point, there would be a review of the artefacts that have been produced so far in the process. Once this review has been completed satisfactorily, the next process can be invoked.

The 'PM set-up' process

The 'identify target PM' activity

Based on the process quagmire, the target process model has been identified as ISO 15288.

The 'identify source PM' activity

Based on the process quagmire, the source process model has been identified as ISO 15504.

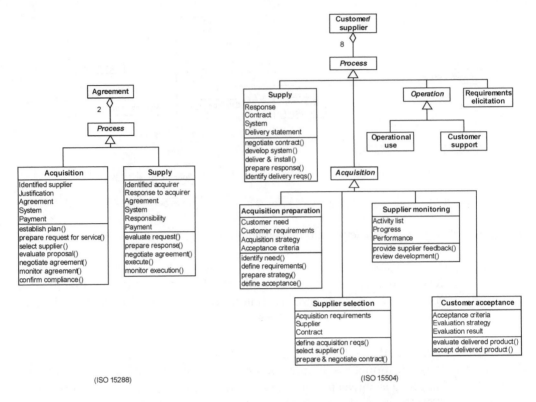

FIGURE 5.16 *Process content views for the standards*

The 'define scope' activity

The next step is to look at the target process model and to identify which processes are to be involved in the mapping exercise. For the sake of brevity for this example, the processes chosen are the ones in the 'Agreement' process group in ISO 15288.

The 'review' activity

As with many processes, there is a review activity at the end of the process that must be passed before progress can be made to the next process from the process instance view.

The 'Process analysis' process

The 'identify gaps' activity

This activity uses the information in Figures 5.14, 5.15 and 5.16 to try to identify any gaps in the mapping between the two standards. Therefore, the question that will be asked is: 'Are there any features of the target process model that do not map onto the source process model?'

The 'identify links' activity

This activity uses the information in Figure 5.14, Figure 5.15 and Figure 5.16 to try to identify any links in the mapping between the two standards. Therefore, the question that will be asked is: 'For each feature of the target process model, which features of the source process model map onto it?'

The 'produce process mapping' activity

This is the activity where the actual results of the previous two activities are recorded. This can be done using any appropriate mechanism and simple tables will be used here to capture the results. This mapping will occur at different levels.

Table 5.1 shows the basic mapping between the two views shown in Figure 5.14. This highlights the differences in the basic language used in both standards. At this level there is a one-to-one mapping for each term, which makes the whole exercise simpler. Once this has been mapped, it is then possible to drop down a level of detail and look at the grouping level.

Table 5.2 shows the mapping between the two views shown in Figure 5.15. This establishes the mapping between the terms used for the process groups and categories. Notice here the first occurrence of a one-to-many mapping between the grouping terms. In ISO 15288, the term 'Project' maps to both 'Support' and 'Management' in ISO 15504.

Table 5.3 shows the mapping between the process terms that are being used in the two standards. Again, there is a one-to-many mapping here where a single term in ISO 15288 ('Acquisition') maps to four terms in ISO 15504.

Table 5.1 *Basic terminology mapping*

ISO 15288	ISO 15504
Process group	Process category
Process	Process
Outcome	Work product
Activity	Practice

Table 5.2 *Process grouping terminology mapping*

ISO 15288		ISO 15504	
Process group	Enterprise	Process category	Organizational
	Agreement		Customer/supplier
	Technical		Engineering
	Project		Management
			Support

Table 5.3 *Process terminology mapping*

ISO 15288		ISO 15504	
Agreement	Acquisition	Customer/supplier	Acquisition preparation
			Supplier selection
			Supplier monitoring
			Customer acceptance
	Supply		Supply

Table 5.4 *Process feature mapping*

ISO 15288		ISO 15504	
Acquisition (outcome)	Identified supplier	Supplier selection	Supplier
	Justification	Supplier selection	Acquisition requirements
	Agreement	Supplier selection	Contract
	System		
	Payment		
Acquisition (activity)	Establish plan	Acquisition preparation	Prepare strategy
	Prepare request for service	Acquisition preparation	Identify needs
			Define requirements
	Select supplier	Supplier selection	Select supplier
	Evaluate proposal	Supplier selection	Select supplier
	Negotiate agreement	Supplier selection	Prepare and negotiate contract
	Monitor agreement	Supplier monitoring	Review development
			Provide supplier feedback
	Confirm compliance	Customer acceptance	Evaluate delivered product
			Accept delivered product
Supply (outcome)	Identified acquirer		
	Response to acquirer	Supply	Response
	Agreement	Supply	Contract
	System	Supply	System
	Responsibility		
	Payment		
Supply (activity)	Evaluate request		
	Prepare response	Supply	Prepare response
	Negotiate agreement	Supply	Negotiate contract
	Execute	Supply	Develop system
			Deliver and install
	Monitor execution		

Table 5.4 shows the mapping between the terms used for the features of the processes – the outcomes and activities of the processes in ISO 15288 to the work products and practices in ISO 15504.

The 'review' activity

Once more, there is a review activity before the process is completed.

The 'Metrics application' process

The 'identify target process' activity

The target process is confirmed as being ISO 15288.

The 'measure PGR' activity

The PGR is calculated by:
> (number of target process groups)/(number of source process groups)

In this case, this is 4:5.

The 'measure PR' activity

The process ratio (PR) is calculated by:
> (number of processes in target process group)/(number of processes in source process group)

In this case, as there is only a single process group, Agreement, selected in the scope, the process ratio is: 2:8.

The 'measure artefact ratio' activity

The artefact ratio is defined as:
> (artefact in target process)/(number of equivalent artefacts in source process)

In this case, the artefact ratios are:

Acquisition	Identified supplier	1:1
	Justification	1:1
	Agreement	1:1
	System	1:0
	Payment	1:0
Supply	Identified acquirer	1:0
	Response to acquirer	1:1
	Agreement	1:1
	System	1:1
	Responsibility	1:0
	Payment	1:0

All these figures are taken from Table 5.4.

The 'measure activity ratio' activity

The activity ratio is defined as:

(activity in target process)/(number of equivalent activities in source process)

In this case, the activity ratios are:

Acquisition	Establish plan	1:1
	Prepare request for service	1:2
	Select supplier	1:1
	Evaluate proposal	1:1
	Negotiate agreement	1:1
	Monitor agreement	1:2
	Confirm compliance	1:2
Supply	Evaluate request	1:0
	Prepare response	1:1
	Negotiate agreement	1:1
	Execute	1:2
	Monitor execution	1:0

All these figures are taken from Table 5.4.

The 'calculate PI' activity

The PI is calculated by:

(number of non-zero artefact ratios + number non-zero activity ratios)/(number artefacts + number activities)

In this case, these are calculated as:

Acquisition PI	$(3 + 7)/(5 + 7) = 10/12 = 0.83$
Supply PI	$(3 + 3)/(6 + 5) = 6/11 = 0.82$

These calculations are based on the figures from the previous section.

The 'calculate PGI' activity

The process group index is calculated as:

(Sum of PI for each process in process group)/(number of processes in process group)

This is calculated as:

Agreement PGI	$(0.83 + 0.82)/2 = 0.825$

These calculations are based on figures from the previous section.

The 'calculate PMI' activity

The process model index is defined as:

(Sum of all PGI)/(total number of PG in the scope)

This is calculated as:

Total PMI   (0.825)/(1) = 0.825

The figures used here are taken from the previous section

The 'review' activity

The final activity in this process is another review, which will evaluate the results of the measurements and metrics applied during this process.

INTERPRETING THE RESULTS

Any metric is useless unless it can be interpreted in some way. The metrics applied in the previous section produced a set of results that can be interpreted according to a set of heuristics, or rules of thumb:

- **PMI of 1**: this means that there is a complete mapping between the target process and the source process. A PMI of 1 does not warrant any further investigation, as the entire process model has a complete mapping. It should be noted that the PMI refers to a mapping in a single direction. Or, to put it another way, a process model index of 1 from target to source does not imply a process model index of 1 from source to target.

- **PMI of under 1**: this implies that there is not a complete mapping between the two process models – the lower the number, the more incomplete the mapping. Therefore this situation needs to be investigated further by looking at the process group indices.

- **PGI of 1**: when each of the process group indices is looked at, any with a value of 1 indicates a complete mapping for that process group and can therefore be ignored for investigation purposes.

- **PGI of under 1**: a process group index of under 1 indicates an incomplete mapping – the lower the number, the more incomplete the mapping. Therefore, any process group with a PGI under 1 should be investigated further by looking at the process indices that went into the calculation.

- **PI of 1**: any processes with a process index of 1 can be ignored for investigation purposes, as this indicates a complete mapping.

- **PI of under 1**: any process that has a process index of under 1 indicates an incomplete mapping for that process. This applies to the artefact ratios and activity ratios that went into the process index calculation. Any artefact ratio or activity ratio that is non-zero will yield the source of the overall mapping incompleteness.

This is by no means an exhaustive list of interpretation of the metrics, but should provide an idea of the sort of use that these metrics can be put to.

CONCLUSIONS

This chapter introduced the concept of process mapping and defined a number of example processes that can be used for such purposes. The processes have been defined according to the process meta-model already introduced in this book. In addition to the mapping processes, an example of a metrics process was defined that used the results of the process mapping processes.

These processes were then illustrated by applying them to a set of standards and identifying a narrow scope of two standards for the example exercise. The processes were executed and the results recorded.

It should be stressed that the processes presented in this chapter are purely for example and should not be taken as the *only* approach to process mapping (although this is a real approach that has been demonstrated on a number of real-life projects). The main purpose here is to illustrate how the process models produced by using the process meta-model can be used as a basis for audit or assessment and any subsequent measurement or metrics exercise.

6 Case Study

'Tiffany Case – definitely distinctive'

James Bond, *Diamonds Are Forever*, UA/Eon/Danjaq

INTRODUCTION

This chapter provides a case study, based on a real organization, where a number of processes are identified and defined according to the meta-model introduced in this book. Particular notice is taken of examples already provided in the book, and some of the approaches taken during the process modelling exercise are discussed.

For reasons of brevity, the case study looks at just a few of the processes in the organization rather than the complete set – a complete process model would probably double the page count of the book. The case study also provides the opportunity for a series of exercises that you can work through at your discretion.

BACKGROUND

The organization under scrutiny is a medium-sized enterprise with approximately 150 employees, and whose main business is the development and support of new products and services for a number of different industries.

The company itself was started as a small enterprise with only five employees. It then grew in size to about 30 members of staff, before being bought out and amalgamated into a larger organization, which is the situation today. This evolution of the organization has resulted in a number of concerns and issues with regards to the processes carried out in the organization, such as:

- The work carried out by the original, small company is mainly concerned with training and support of the products that are developed by the rest of the company. Because the company started out as a few like-minded individuals, there were very few, if any, processes defined, as everyone had a good appreciation (or so they thought) of the work carried out by all other employees. Although this worked out fine when there were only a few people, as the company grew, the communication issues between the various members of staff

117

increased enormously and it was only when the takeover occurred that the truth of the lack of process truly struck home.

- The main work carried out by the larger arm of the organization was split into two main camps – the technical camp and the sales camp. The technical camp was made up of engineers, scientists and support technicians who worked on the conception and development of new products. The ideas for new developments came directly from the sales and marketing staff who were, on the whole, non-technical people who had a terrible habit of promising the world to customers without understanding whether the promised goods and services were feasible either in terms of technology or the timescales involved. Also, the semantic gap between the technical and non-technical staff often resulted in the wrong system being delivered to the customer.

- On top of all these problems, some customers started to insist on something called 'quality', which was a new concept to the organization. Therefore, a quality team was hastily put together comprising project managers, who were then assigned the task of bringing the company's quality up-to-scratch, as quickly as possible and with limited resources. Indeed, several large customers from both the medical and transport industries decided that independent auditors would be brought in to ensure that the products and services offered met particular industry and international standards.

These are not insignificant problems. However, they are also very real problems that occur within many organizations, large, medium or small, and represent a typical set of problems.

The initial reaction to ensuring quality was to get an independent auditor in to carry out a pre-audit to see at what stage the company was, in terms of maturity of processes. This resulted in an anti-climax, as the formal auditor simply declared that as no processes were formally documented, it was impossible to carry out a proper pre-audit. The auditor advised the company to save their money and not bother with a full, formal audit until things had changed significantly.

At this point, when the perception was that all was lost, somebody made the point that the company must actually have processes that were executed successfully, otherwise the organization would not produce anything and would have no customers. The conclusion was, therefore, that the processes must be hidden and that they needed to be captured and then documented, which would keep the auditors happy.

The resulting action, therefore, was to apply process modelling to see how it could help the organization.

THE APPROACH

As has been stated already, there are many starting points for process modelling and deciding what to do first is often the most difficult part of the whole approach. Remember that the overall intention is to generate a complete process description based on the process meta-model and this process model has seven views. Therefore there are seven different start points to choose from, depending on what information is already known to the modeller. A good piece of advice is always to start where you have some information or, better still, an understanding of some aspect of the process. Each of the seven view points is discussed in turn below, with a few possible reasons why each particular view may be chosen as the start point.

- **Process content view**: this is a good starting point when there is some evidence of a documented process in the organization. Processes can be identified, their artefacts and activities captured and then this information used to drive the rest of the project. This is often the starting point when conducting an audit or assessment against some sort of standard.

- **Process structure view**: similarly, the process structure view can be a good start point where there is an existing, or partial, process model.

- **Process behaviour view**: the process behaviour view is a popular view to begin with where there are hidden processes that have been carried out by individuals over a period of time, yet there is no documentation. If you ask someone how they do something, the usual response is to describe a series of simple steps that equate to the process behaviour view. This is often the start point when talking with the people who actually carry out the processes, rather than managers of the process. This view can also be useful for gaining a consensus of opinion between different people who work on either the same process or on two processes that interact in some way.

- **Stakeholder view**: often, especially when dealing with managers, people will start to describe either the people or (more correctly) the roles of people in the organization and then use this as a starting point to find out who is responsible for what sort of activities.

- **Information view**: this is a good place to start when there is very little process description yet there is evidence of artefacts being produced, such as design specifications, minutes from meetings, test results, and so on. It is possible to start to identify processes based on the information that has been produced on a particular project or from a particular section of the work force.

- **Requirements view**: very often people want to forget about the actual processes and oncentrate on what it is that they are trying to achieve by the process modelling exercise. In such circumstances, the requirements view can be a very good place to start the process modelling.

- **Process instance view**: the process instance, although not a common start point, can be used to generate the rest of the model when someone is describing an overall life cycle of a project. Very often, rather than talking about real phases of projects, people will often (confusingly and incorrectly) be talking about processes. In such situations, then the process instance view is a good start point for the generation of the whole process model.

Bear in mind also that it is possible to have more than one starting point. Consider the organization in the case study, where the single enterprise has grown from two separate sources. In this case, the information known about the processes will fall into two distinct camps.

Once a process model has a starting point, it is possible to see which other views are related to it in some way and, hence, the whole of the meta-model can then be navigated, captured and populated. The consistency checks that were presented in Chapter 4 are a very good means of understanding where to go next with the process modelling.

INTERPRETING THE PROCESS MODEL

When considering the process model, it is important to be able to read and understand the processes that are being described. This may seem obvious from the whole tone of this book, but there are far more benefits that may be obtained by thinking again about the content of the process model, for example:

- **Identifying complexity**: it has already been established that complexity is one of the three 'evils of life' (see Chapter 4) and that it is important to be able to identify and, hence, control it, but the reason why complexity exists can be very useful. Suppose a process behaviour view is created that is very complex; it is easy to see that complexity exists – the diagram will be messy and difficult to understand. However, it is worth finding out what the original source information for the diagram was – was it legacy information, or information that was created from scratch? If the answer is that the process has been started from scratch with a blank sheet of paper, then the process *must* be redefined, as the complexity has crept in through the fault of the person designing the process. This is what Brooks refers to as *accidental* complexity that can be avoided (Brooks, 1995). The other option, of course, is that the process model is based on an existing process, in which case the answer is not as simple, as it may not be possible to change the nature of the processes themselves. In such cases, the complexity is not the fault of the process modeller, as the complexity is inherent in the system. This is what Brooks refers to as *essential* complexity as it is in the essence of the system (Brooks, 1995).

- **Sanity checking**: it is possible to use the process model as a sanity check to ensure that the whole model fits together and, at the end of the day, that it makes sense. It is perfectly possible to have a well-defined process model but one that makes no logical sense to any of the users. The key view to consider here is the requirements view, which is setting the scene for the whole process model and will form the basic sense of the system.

- **Business analysis**: once the model exists, all sorts of analysis techniques may be applied. For example, the process model may be examined for efficiency, usually by looking at the behavioural aspect of the process model. For example, individual processes may be analysed for complexity by considering the process behaviour view, whereas the overall efficiency may be examined by considering the process instance view.

This is by no means an exhaustive list, but gives a general idea about the different ways that the process model may be considered and used.

The process model for the case study is introduced in the next section and, as each view is considered, some of these interpretation issues will be used as discussion points.

THE CASE STUDY PROCESS MODEL

The process model for the case study consists of the seven views from the process meta-model. The views are presented here in no particular order.

Process structure view

The process structure view for the case study is shown in Figure 6.1 and defines the basic structure and terminology to be used in the process model.

The diagram in Figure 6.1 shows the process content view which includes the basic structure of the process model and the types of process group that have been identified. The basic terms that are used to define a process are:

- **Artefact**: describes any input or output of a process. Artefacts may include: reports, documents, minutes, components of the system, the system, specifications and so on. The actual artefacts themselves are described in the information view.

- **Activity**: describes the steps involved in the process or the things that must be done in order to execute the process correctly. Activities produce and consume artefacts.

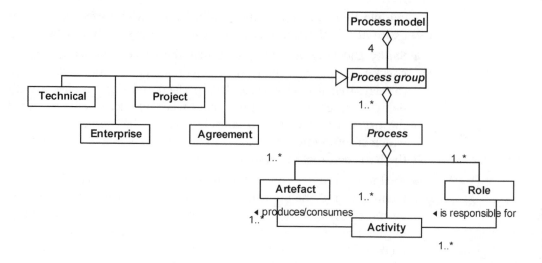

FIGURE 6.1 *Process structure view*

- **Role**: describes the stakeholder role that is responsible for the various activities. All activities must have an associated role.

All processes are categorized according to four process groups, which have been identified as:

- **Agreement**: describes all processes that relate to the customer–supplier relationship with the organization.
- **Project**: describes all processes associated with management and support within the organization.
- **Technical**: describes all processes associated with development and engineering activities within the organization
- **Enterprise**: describes all the processes that apply across the whole of the organization.

The actual processes within each group are identified and described by the process content view for each of the process categories.

The process structure view also forms the basis for the high-level mapping to any source standards or process models that may be relevant to the organization.

Process content view

The process content view describes the actual processes that are contained within each of the process groups identified in the process structure view. As is often the case in real-life process models, this amounts to a number of processes and, therefore, it is usual to split the view into several lower-level views. An obvious choice for partitioning this split is to base each of the lower-level views on one of the process groups. Therefore, in this case there will be at least four basic views that make up the entire process content view. It is possible, and likely, that there will eventually be more than four views as, in some cases, there may be a lot of processes within a single view, particularly when it comes to describing the core capability of the organization by its processes. For example, an organization that is predominately concerned with managing projects is likely to have a complex process content view for the 'Project' process group, whereas an organization more focused on, say, product development, will have a more complex process content view for the 'technical' process group.

In some cases, it is common for one or more of the process groups to be further divided into lower-level groups. In the example in this case study, the 'Project' process group has been subdivided into two other groups: 'Management' and 'Support', as shown in Figure 6.2. Although this is fine in theory, caution must be exercised that too many levels are not introduced, which will lead to an increase in the complexity of the model. As a simple rule-of-thumb, it is a good idea to minimize the number of levels of process group to two or three nested levels, in other words, no more than in the example shown in Figure 6.2.

Now that the process groups have been subdivided, it is possible to look inside each one and see what processes exist and what associated artefacts and activities (using the terminology here) exist for each process.

Figure 6.3 shows the first of the process content views, for the 'Enterprise' process group. Remember that these processes are ones that will apply across the whole of the organization and are, therefore, applicable to everyone within the company.

Figure 6.3 shows the processes that have been identified for the 'Enterprise' process category and the first thing that springs to mind is

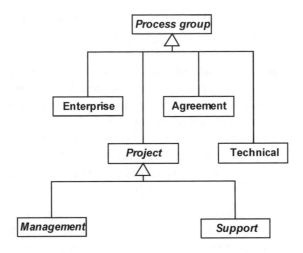

FIGURE 6.2 *Further breakdown of the 'Project' process group*

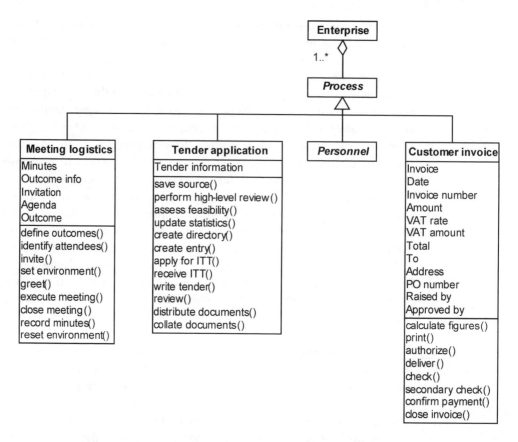

FIGURE 6.3 *Process content view for the 'Enterprise' process group*

that there are not many processes in this group. This could be for a number of reasons:

- Bear in mind that the company in question has grown from two small companies into a single larger company. In situations like this it is not uncommon for there to be a lack of enterprise-level processes. In a small organization, there tends to be more emphasis on the technical and management-related processes than on higher-level processes that apply to the core business. Conversely, some large organizations have many more of these high-level processes defined and fewer technical and management ones. This can often reflect the distribution of roles in the organization – too many levels of management often result in a top-heavy process model that leans towards enterprise-level processes.

- As the process modelling initiative has only just started, there are no processes in place that actually relate to process modelling or process improvement. This is to be expected in such a scenario but, if the

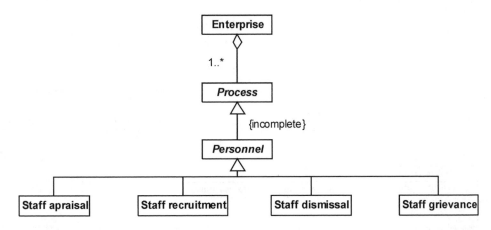

FIGURE 6.4 *Process content view for 'Enterprise' with an emphasis on 'Personnel'*

process content view was to be examined in, say, six months' time, you would certainly expect to see more high-level processes relating to process modelling and/or process improvement.

- The company itself is still relatively small. Perhaps it does not have a dedicated personnel department, hence the lack of employment-related processes. In fact, the only process that relates directly to employees here is the 'Personnel' process, which is broken down in Figure 6.4.

Although four 'Personnel' processes have been identified in Figure 6.4, none of them has any artefacts or activities defined. In this situation, it so happened that the area of 'Personnel' processes was identified as being very weak, therefore a set of processes was identified, but not fully. This can serve two useful purposes. The first is that it demonstrates to a third party that, although no processes exist at the moment, the whole area has not been overlooked but is waiting for attention. The other purpose is to remind the process modellers that the model is still incomplete. It is possible that if these empty processes did not exist, someone would assume that the process model was complete, as all processes that exist have been populated.

Note the use of the '{incomplete}' constraint here to indicate that there are more processes on the same level as 'Personnel' not shown here.

As with all views in the process meta-model, it is important to look not just at what processes are present, but also which processes are missing from the process model. When carrying out business-related analysis exercises, the lack of processes is often as revealing as the presence of processes and can give a good indication of the focus of the organization and where areas of knowledge exist.

The next group to be examined is the 'Technical' process group.

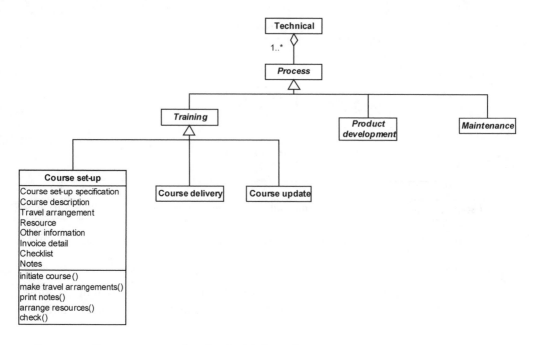

FIGURE 6.5 *Process content view for the 'Technical' process group, with an emphasis on the 'Training' processes*

Figure 6.5 shows the process content view for the 'Technical' process group but, as much of the emphasis of this organization is on product development and training, the process group has been split into three main subdivisions, which are:

- **Training**: describes processes related to training activities. These processes are based on the original, small company that was purely devoted to training.

- **Product development**: focuses on the development of new products. This has originated from the parent organization that bought out the smaller company.

- **Maintenance**: focuses on the maintenance of products that are in the market place and, again, was originated from the parent organization.

It should be clear from this summary of the subdivisions that there is a potential for problems in integrating these processes that have originated from two different sources.

There are three processes that have been identified that are associated with training, each with different levels of detail defined. These are:

- **Course set-up**: describes the activities involved in making sure that all the preparations have been made to run a successful course.

- **Course delivery**: describes how the course itself must be delivered. This includes not only course delivery, but also monitoring of the course and how the tutor must behave towards attendees (greeting, introductions, and so on).

- **Course update**: allows feedback to be taken from the course and then used as a basis for improvements and enhancements to future courses. It also allows for any mistakes or ambiguities that were highlighted during the course delivery to be fed back into the system.

Figure 6.6 emphasizes the technical processes associated with product development and the first impression is one of surprise at how many process there are. This is clearly indicative of an organization with a strong history of product development and one that has quite a level of understanding of the processes involved. There are two interesting things to notice about this view:

- The processes identified reflect the typical processes described by many technical life cycle models. The processes of requirements,

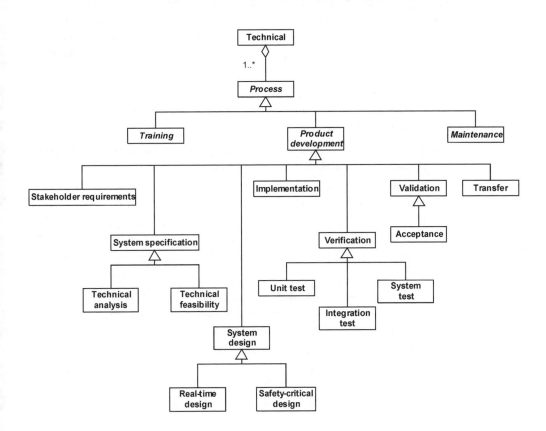

FIGURE 6.6 *Process content view for the 'Technical' process group, with an emphasis on 'Product development'*

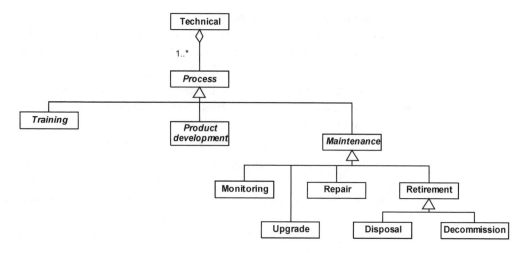

FIGURE 6.7 *Process content view for the 'Technical' process group, with an emphasis on 'Maintenance' processes*

specification and design will be familiar to many engineers and will form the backbone of any sort of development.

- Several of the processes have been tailored for slightly different approaches to meet the same process. For example, the 'Design' process, the 'System specification' process and the 'Verification' process.

Figure 6.7 shows the technical processes once again, but this time emphasizes the maintenance processes within the organization. There are two aspects of this view that are of interest:

- There is a focus on the operations of the product and, hence, any error reporting activities that need to be executed.

- There is also a focus on the eventual retirement of the system. This is often indicative of the organization taking a responsible view towards its products. Indeed, many organizations do not even consider what happens to their products once they have reached the end of their life cycle. In this example, there is not one, but two options for retiring the system:

  - The 'Decommission' process, which describes how to take a system out of action. It may then be left in existence or, indeed, disposed of, as described by the next process.

  - The 'Disposal' process, which describes how to get rid of the product in a responsible way. In fact, as the world becomes more and more environmentally aware of the fact that something must happen when systems 'die', this is an encouraging sign within an organization.

By considering these processes, think about what sort of products this company may be involved in producing. If any harmful substances were involved, then one would expect to see far more processes identified for disposal. There is no mention of recycling here, so this may mean that there is little opportunity for recycling or, in a worse scenario, that the organization has not considered recycling for the products.

Figures 6.8 and 6.9 concentrate on the 'Project' process group and look at the various processes that are used within the organization.

Figure 6.8 shows the process content view for the 'Project' process group (which has two main types: 'Management' and 'Support') and this diagram concentrates on the 'Management' processes.

There are three management-related processes that have been identified:

- **Project scheduling**: describes the process for generating the initial project schedule and project plan.

- **Project monitoring**: describes the process for monitoring the project once it has started and that continues until completion.

- **Project review**: describes a review process that may be invoked periodically throughout the project to ensure that, for example, project gates can be passed effectively.

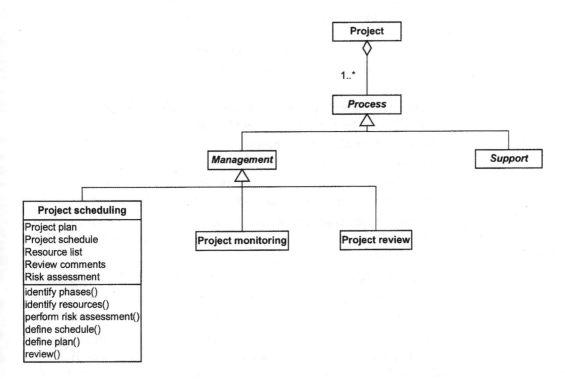

FIGURE 6.8 *Process content view for the 'Project' process group, with an emphasis on 'Management'*

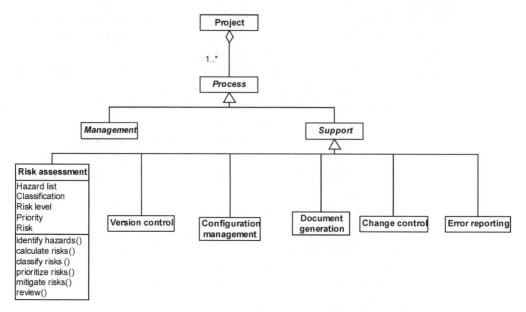

FIGURE 6.9 *Process content view for the 'Project' process group, with an emphasis on 'Support'*

On the whole, you might consider this part of the process content view to be fairly lightweight, as three is not a huge number. Again, rather than simply reading the diagram, it is worth looking beneath the surface of the model and considering why there are few processes for project management.

Figure 6.9 shows the same process content view but, this time, with an emphasis on the 'Support' processes. There are six support processes identified:

- **Risk assessment**: potential hazards are identified and the risk classified, prioritized and mitigated against.

- **Version control**: the mechanisms for identifying all artefacts in a unique way is defined.

- **Configuration management**: covers how the different versions of artefacts are managed and controlled, including build control.

- **Document generation**: covers how documents must be created and describes any templates or structures that must be used in the documents themselves.

- **Change control**: defines the identification and execution of changes.

- **Error reporting**: covers the mechanisms for identifying, reporting and resolving errors that may occur at any point in the process.

Again, these processes have been identified but not yet defined, which shows that, although the definitions are missing, the organization is aware of this omission. When such omissions occur, it is worth trying to understand why they occur in the first place. There could be several reasons for a pattern in the process model like this to occur in the management area, such as:

- **Engineers as project managers**: in a company that has evolved from a small group of engineers, such as this one, it is common to find out that all the project management roles are being carried out by engineers who are also working on the development of the project. This can often result in an emphasis on the engineering activities, rather than the management activities, as is the case here.

- **Small or short-term projects**: very often, small projects or projects with a short timeframe exhibit a lack of management processes. This may be because the perception is that there is not enough time for management, or perhaps more informal, agile management techniques are being implemented.

- **Small project teams**: in some cases, it may be that the number of people working on a project is very small, or is in fact just a single person. In such situations, management practices are often non-existent, as the communication tends to be, or is perceived to be, very strong. However, when these projects increase in size and more people are assigned, this lack of management processes becomes very apparent. Although an informal approach to management may seem adequate when few people are involved, it falls apart when the project is scaled up.

- **Slackness or arrogance**: of course, the most obvious reason why there are few management processes could simply be due to slackness or arrogance on behalf of the project personnel. If the project staff have no real motivation, this can result in slackness, whereas if the project team have an inflated opinion of their abilities, this can result in arrogance. Another cause of arrogance is when someone (it is usually a single person) views themselves as a 'project champion' who can turn a bad or failing project around through their own project prowess, immortality and general greatness of being. Unfortunately, these causes are nowhere near as uncommon as they should be.

These are not all of the reasons for a dearth of management processes, but it provides an indication that the patterns manifested in the process model should be thought about, rather than just read and accepted.

Figure 6.10 shows the process content view for the 'Agreement' process group, which has four processes identified:

- **Project initiation**: concerned with making the initial contact with the customer, defining the initial requirements for the project and coming up with the original agreement or contract.

- **Project monitoring**: once a problem is up and running, it should be continuously monitored to ensure that it is both on schedule and still meeting its original requirements.

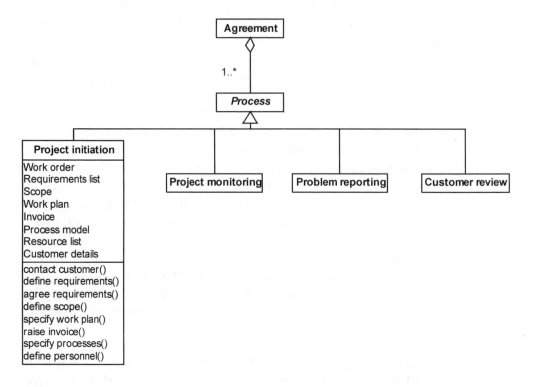

FIGURE 6.10 *Process content view for the 'Agreement' process group*

- **Problem reporting**: when problems do occur, which is inevitable, then it is important that they can be picked up and dealt with effectively.

- **Customer review**: it is important that not only the project team thinks that they have executed a successful project, but also that the customer does as well. These reviews may be periodical throughout the course of the project (particularly where long projects are concerned) and also at the end of the project as part of the final acceptance.

This completes the process content view, which can often turn out to be one of the largest views in the project.

Stakeholder view

The stakeholder view is concerned with identifying all the roles in the organization. If the process behaviour view or the requirements view already exist, then they can be a good source for identifying stakeholders.

The stakeholder view itself is shown in the Figures 6.11, 6.12 and 6.13.

Figure 6.11 shows the stakeholder view with an emphasis on 'Customer'. These stakeholders are described as follows:

- **Sponsor**: describes the role of the person or organization who will, ultimately, be funding any work.

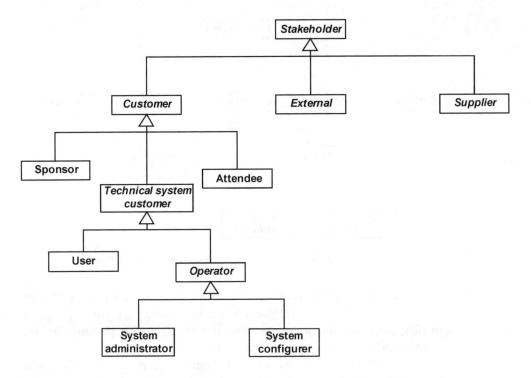

FIGURE 6.11 *Stakeholder view with an emphasis on 'Customer'*

- **Technical system customer**: an abstract role that serves as a simple grouping.
- **User**: Represents the role of the end-users of the system being produced.
- **Operator**: another abstract role, which groups together all types of people who will operate the system.
- **System administrator**: represents the role of the people who will be responsible for controlling the final system.
- **System configurer**: represents the role of the people who will be responsible for the installation and set-up of the final system.

Figure 6.12 identifies the stakeholder roles associated with 'External'. The roles are described in more detail as follows:

- **Standards**: represents a grouping of all roles relating to standards.
- **Standard provider**: represents the role of the organizations who produce standards, such as the BSI, ISO, and so on.
- **Standard enforcer**: represents the role of all those involved with independent audits and assessments.
- **Safety enforcer**: represents the role of all those involved with safety assurance for the products.

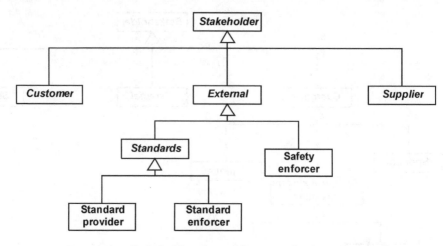

FIGURE 6.12 *Stakeholder view with an emphasis on 'External'*

Figure 6.13 shows all the roles associated with the 'Supplier' class. Rather than go into detail about all these roles, as there are many, we will discuss the diagram from the point of view of looking at the patterns in the diagram and comparing them to previous ones.

This first thing that stands out with Figure 6.13 is that it is far more complex than Figures 6.11 or 6.12. This is only to be expected as there are usually far more roles that can be identified within an organization than outside it. This is because people will usually have a better understanding of their own organization than of others.

There are two main groupings here: 'Technical' and 'Management'. Notice the difference between the number of technical roles that have

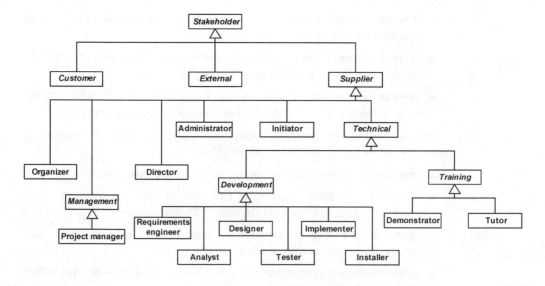

FIGURE 6.13 *Stakeholder view with an emphasis on 'Supplier'*

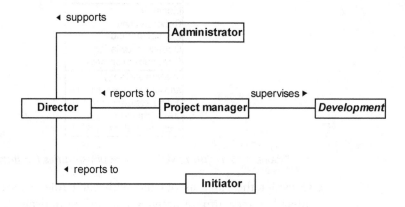

FIGURE 6.14 *Enhancing stakeholders with additional relationships*

been identified (in fact, this is divided into two further groups) compared to the management roles (a single role – 'Project manager'). This can be explained by the background of the company having originally few employees and most of those with a technical background.

Further investigation of the 'Technical' role reveals that it is split between 'Training' and 'Development', which mirrors the main capabilities of the original companies.

The roles that do not fall into either of these categories also bear consideration. It is tempting to put all of these roles into another grouping but caution must be exercised as some of these roles are not similar enough to be grouped together. The other temptation is to create a generic grouping called something like 'Other roles' to serve as a general catch-all. Although this seems quite sensible, it can often lead to people being lazy and simply putting any role that has not been thought about into the same category.

Extending the stakeholder view

The stakeholder view can be extended to add extra value to the process model in three different ways, as follows:

- Tie it into a more traditional organizational chart. It is possible, for example, to start to add relationships between the various roles that can form the basis for an organizational chart. Figure 6.14 shows how the stakeholder view may be extended by considering the relationship between the various roles, rather than just the classification of roles. This can be used as a driver for, or indeed part of the analysis of, an organizational chart. Typical relationships that can be shown on such an extended view include: 'reports to', 'supports' and 'supervises'.

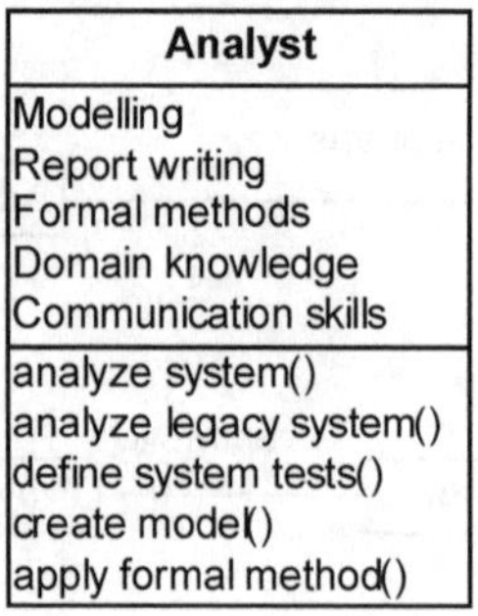

Analyst
Modelling
Report writing
Formal methods
Domain knowledge
Communication skills
analyze system()
analyze legacy system()
define system tests()
create model()
apply formal method()

FIGURE 6.15 *Defining skills and responsibilities for stakeholders*

- Consider the skills associated with each role. This is important for areas like recruitment activities or staff appraisals. It is important to understand the skills required by each stakeholder and can be a powerful way to ensure that the stakeholder name is an appropriate one. In terms of representing this information on the model, this is quite straightforward, as skills may be thought of as a list of features that the role must exhibit, which means that they can be represented on the stakeholder class by simply populating the class attributes for the stakeholder.

- Associate responsibilities for each role. Providing that the process behaviour view exists, then this is a simple step as it is simply a matter of identifying all processes with a particular role as a swim lane name, and then abstracting the activities that it is responsible for. This can also be represented very simply on the model by creating a list of class operations for each stakeholder.

Figure 6.15 shows an example of how the skills and responsibilities of a stakeholder may be represented visually on the model as attributes and operations respectively.

Requirements view

The requirements view captures the driving needs behind the processes. There will be several diagrams that comprise the requirements view depending on the nature of the organization. Potentially, there may be more than one requirements view for each process, as each process will be viewed differently by each stakeholder. In order to minimize the number of diagrams in the requirements view, while still capturing enough business knowledge, it is important to consider each diagram carefully.

For this case study, we consider two main areas of work – training and invoicing. First, we consider the company's training-related processes.

Training

Figure 6.5 identified a number of processes related to the company training capability, which were identified as: 'Course set-up', Course

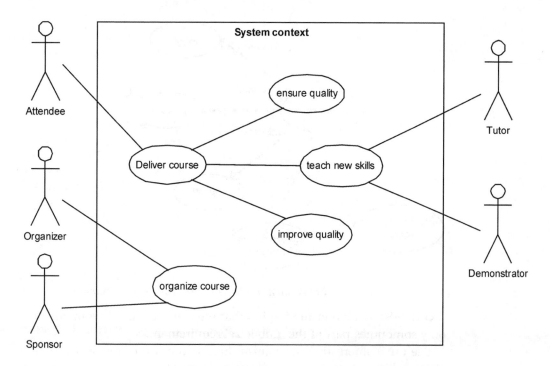

FIGURE 6.16 *Simple context for training-related processes*

delivery' and 'Course update', but the question to be answered here is 'why?' The company requirements for the training capability need to be identified, as shown in Figure 6.16.

Figure 6.16 shows a simple context for training-related processes. There are two main requirements shown here: 'deliver course' and 'organize course'. 'Deliver course' is related in some way to three other require-ments: 'ensure quality', 'teach new skills' and 'improve quality'. Notice that this diagram has not been fully populated in terms of the relationship as, at the moment, these are all represented as simple lines, rather than the more meaningful relationships discussed in Chapter 2.

It is quite common to consider one of these high-level requirements in more detail by decomposing it into lower-level requirements on another diagram, as shown in Figure 6.17, which shows a decomposition of the 'Organize course' requirement. Notice how this diagram is more mean-ingful as the relationships are more explicit between the various requirements.

There is one main requirement identified here, 'organize course', which has three included requirements: 'set up', 'publicize' and 'support'. The '<<includes>>' relationship implies that these three requirements are always part of the main requirement. There is also an extension to the 'publicize' requirement that has been identified as 'cancel course' The

137

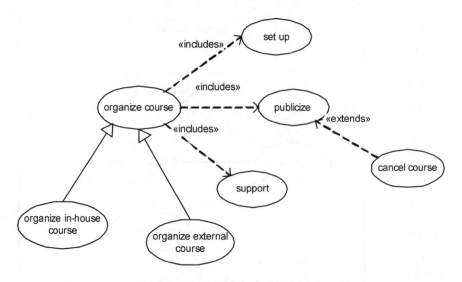

FIGURE 6.17 *Breakdown of the 'Organize course' requirement*

'<<extends>>' relationship implies that the 'cancel course' requirement is only sometimes part of the 'publicize' requirement.

The other interesting mechanism here is the use of the specialization relationship, as 'organize course' has two types: 'organize in-house course' and 'organize external course'. What is interesting here is that both of these specializations inherit the structure from their parent requirement.

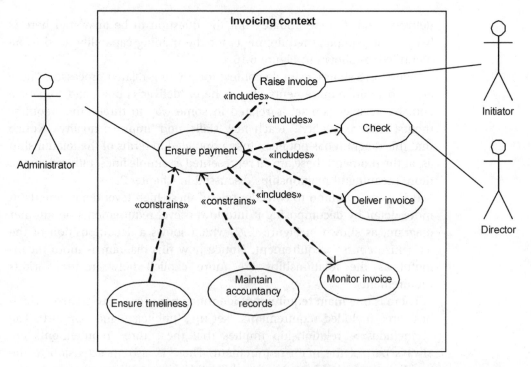

FIGURE 6.18 *Requirements view for invoice-related processes*

Therefore, both 'organize in-house course' and 'organize external course' include: 'set up', 'publicize' and 'support'.

Invoicing

As our second example of a requirements view, consider Figure 6.18, which shows the requirements view for invoice-related processes. Note here that the main requirement, 'Ensure payment' has four included requirements: 'Raise invoice', 'Check', 'Deliver invoice' and 'Monitor invoice'. Also note here that the main requirement has two constraints upon it: 'Ensure timeliness' and 'Maintain accountancy records'.

The validation of these requirements by the processes from the process content are demonstrated in the process instance view.

Information view

The information view shows the artefacts that are present in the process model and, just as importantly, it also shows the relationships between them. The information model may be split over different levels of abstraction. It is quite common to have an overall information model that shows the high-level artefacts and the conceptual relationships between them, but then to also break down each artefact into more detail

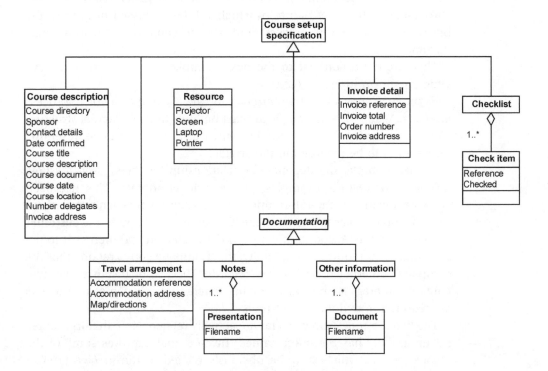

FIGURE 6.19 *Information view for the 'Course set-up' process artefacts*

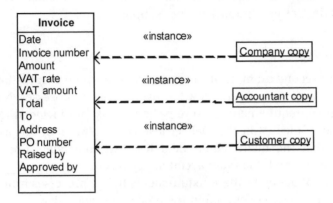

FIGURE 6.20 *Information view for the 'Customer invoice' process artefacts*

and to describe the exact content and structure of each one. Figure 6.19 focuses on the artefacts for a single process – the 'Course set-up' process.

Figure 6.19 shows the main artefact for the 'Course set-up' process discussed previously. This diagram is particularly interesting, as there is only a single main artefact, 'Course set-up specification'. Although the artefact itself is relatively complex, all the information generated as part of the artefact is gathered into a single entity, in this case it is actually realized by a document. Different parts of the document are generated by different stakeholders (the exact nature of which will be discussed in the process behaviour view for this process) and they all come together in a single document.

This is quite a contrast to the next example of an information view, which is shown in Figure 6.20.

Figure 6.20 shows the main artefact for the 'Customer invoice' process artefacts. Again, there is a single artefact but, this time, the actual structure of the information is quite simple – just a list of attributes representing information to be recorded in the artefact.

In this example, the dependency relationship has been used to show instances, or real-life examples, of the process artefact. This has been shown explicitly on the information, as for each invoice generated, there must be three copies printed out: the 'Customer copy' sent to the customer for payment; the 'Accountant copy', initially retained and then sent to the accountants as required; and, finally, the 'Company copy', retained for the company's internal book-keeping records. The use of instances is quite common in areas such as accountancy where multiple copies of artefacts are required to maintain audit trails.

The two examples shown so far are actually related. Note that the course set-up artefact has a section named 'Invoice' that captures some of the invoice details, which is, quite obviously related to the invoice artefact itself. Indeed, the 'Invoice' artefact is related to a number of other artefacts

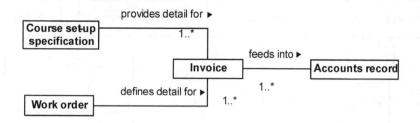

FIGURE 6.21 *Information view relating artefacts*

from other processes that must be identified in order to ensure that the process model is consistent and that the processes will work together when executed (this is further explored in the discussion of the process instance view). Figure 6.21 illustrates this.

Figure 6.21 shows how higher-level artefacts from different processes can be related together in the information view. It is these higher-level relationships that verify that the processes will work with one another, in terms of their inputs, outputs and general information consistency. The artefacts shown here are from the following processes: 'Course set-up', 'Customer invoice', 'Project initiation' and an, as-yet undefined, accounts-related process.

Process instance view

The process instance view forms the heart of the validation of the processes that are defined in the process model. As has already been discussed, the requirements for a set of processes are likely to change as time goes on, therefore it is essential that there is a mechanism for validating each requirement. The basic mechanism of the process instance view is to validate a particular requirement, or set of requirements, by executing a number of processes that have been identified in the process content view and seeing whether they meet the desired capability of the requirements.

In the following two examples, the 'Ensure payment' requirement from Figure 6.18 will be chosen as the requirement to be validated. For any requirement, there are always a number of ways that the requirement can be met that manifest themselves into a sequence of processes; in other words, a number of scenarios may be defined for each requirement. The following two diagrams show two different scenarios for the same requirement that allow the requirements to be validated by executing a number of different processes.

Figure 6.22 shows the process instance view that represent a scenario for normal operation of a project and invoicing. In this example, the first process to be instantiated, or executed, is that of 'Project initiation'. This then invokes the 'Meeting logistics' process, which in turn invokes the

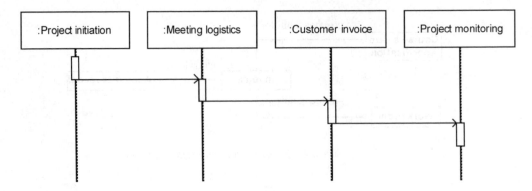

FIGURE 6.22 *Process instance view for the 'Ensure payment' requirement for a normal project scenario*

'Customer invoice' process and, finally, the 'Project monitoring' process. The execution of these processes in this particular sequence represents how a normal project is run and also validates that the 'Customer invoice' process is correctly executed during the course of a normal project. There are, however, a number of other scenarios in which the 'Customer invoice' process may be required, another of which is described in the scenario below.

Figure 6.23 again shows a scenario for the 'Ensure payment' requirement but, in this instance, the scenario represents how a course is set up, delivered and invoiced. As can be seen from the diagram, the order of process execution is: (i) 'Project initiation' as in the previous scenario; (ii) 'Course set up'; (iii) 'Customer invoice'; and (iv) 'Course delivery'.

Another option with the process instance view that can greatly help with validating the stakeholders is to include instances of these stakeholders on the diagram.

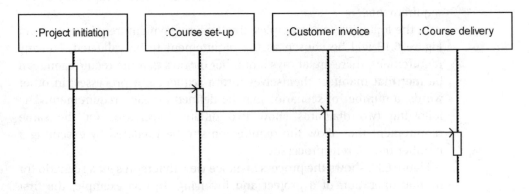

FIGURE 6.23 *Process instance view for the 'Ensure payment' requirement for the scenario of running a course*

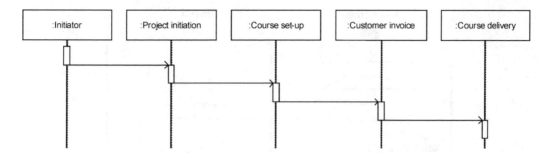

FIGURE 6.24 *Process instance view including stakeholder instance*

Figure 6.24 shows the same scenario as in Figure 6.23, but this time an instance of a stakeholder has been identified and included as a life line.

The number of scenarios required by a single requirement is potentially infinite, as there are countless possibilities. Creating scenarios is analogous to testing in that there is no limit to the amount of testing that can be carried out. It is important to execute enough scenarios that provide sufficient coverage for the requirements while providing a level of confidence that the processes will work effectively.

Process behaviour view

The process behaviour view describes how each process is executed in terms of its activities, artefacts and responsibilities. The process behaviour view can often be the start point of a process modelling exercise, particularly where information is to be extracted from inside someone's head and reproduced on paper. The process behaviour view has very strong links to the process content view and for each process identified, there must exist a process behaviour view. The process behaviour view is realized using an activity diagram that will be a 'comfortable' view to many people as it looks like, and indeed has its origins in, a flowchart diagram.

Figure 6.25 shows how the 'Customer invoice' process is executed in terms of the order of execution of the activities and the production and consumption of artefacts by each activity. Also, note how responsibility for each activity has been allocated using swim lanes that are themselves related to stakeholders from the stakeholder view.

Figure 6.26 shows the process behaviour view for the 'Course set-up' process. Of interest in this diagram is the use of UML signals, represented graphically by an irregular pentagon, to indicate that a message is being sent to another part of the model. In this case, the signals are showing messages that start off other processes. The first signal, 'raise invoice', is sent once the course has been initiated and it kicks off the 'Customer invoice' process. This is a good way to show the relationships between processes that are tightly coupled.

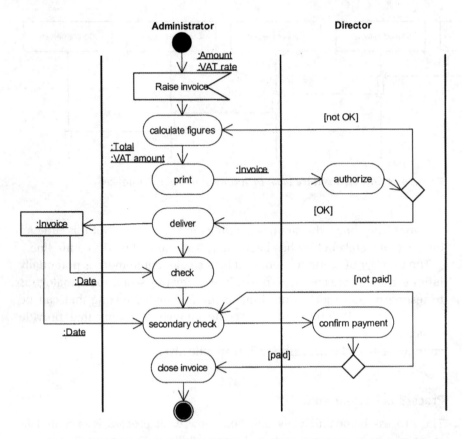

FIGURE 6.25 *Process behaviour view for the 'Customer invoice' process*

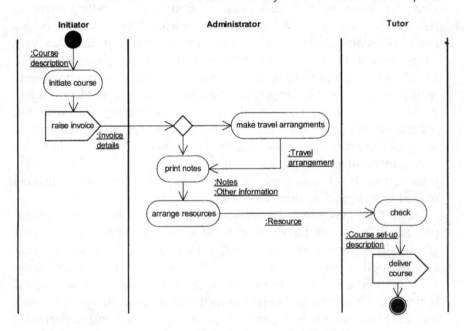

FIGURE 6.26 *Process behaviour view for the 'Course set-up' process*

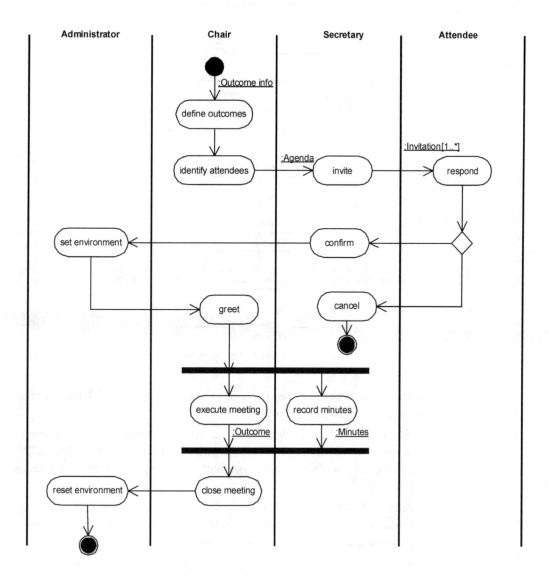

FIGURE 6.27 *Process behaviour view for the 'Meeting logistics' process*

Figure 6.27 shows the process behaviour view for the 'Meeting logistics' process. Of interest here is a control split and join, but notice this time how the responsibility for each of the concurrent activities is controlled by different swim lanes.

PROCESS MAPPING

The process model that has been generated so far, as was stated in the introduction, will be used ultimately as the source for various standard assessments. To give a broad idea of how this model maps onto source

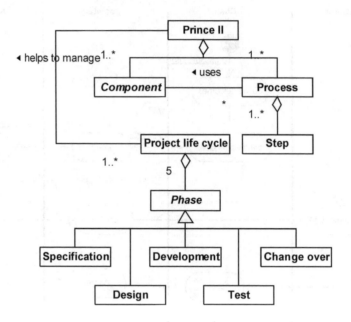

FIGURE 6.28 *Process structure view for Prince II*

standards, we take two standards as a simple example of basic process mapping. These two standards are:

- **ISO 15288**: a generic systems standard for systems life cycle management that can be applied to almost any project. Although ISO 15288 covers all process areas, it is particularly strong in the technical areas (ISO, 2002).
- **Prince II**: for projects in a controlled environment. This is a process model that is used extensively on UK government projects and that is focused primarily on management issues (Bentley, 2001).

Table 6.1 *Initial mapping between ISO 15288 and Prince II*

ISO 15288	Prince II
Life cycle	Project life cycle
Process group	
Conception	Specification
Development	Design
Construction	Development
	Test
Transition	Change over
Operations	
Retirement	

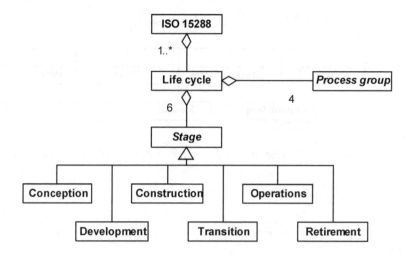

FIGURE 6.29 *Process structure view for ISO 15288*

Figure 6.28 shows the process structure view for Prince II, which provides a good overview of the whole standard. It can be seen that there are two main elements that go to make up the Prince II process model – 'Component' and 'Process'. The Prince II process model helps to manage a 'Project life cycle' that is made up of five types of 'Phase', which are: 'Specification', 'Design', 'Development', 'Test' and 'Change over'.

Figure 6.29 shows a similar-looking process structure for ISO 15288. If an initial mapping between the two process models is considered, the mappings listed in Table 6.1 emerge. In some cases, the mapping is quite obvious, as the terminology used is very similar. For example, 'Life cycle' and 'Project life cycle' are similar terms and they do indeed map. Caution must be exercised, however, as some terms, although they appear similar, or the same, actually represent different concepts. As an example of this, consider the term 'Development' that is used in both process models to describe a particular type of phase. At first glance, this appears to be a straightforward mapping, but when taken in the context of the other mappings, it is clear that they are fundamentally different. In ISO 15288, the development stage is concerned with analysing the problem and producing an optimum design, whereas in Prince II, the development phase is more concerned with constructing the system, with all the analysis and design activities having been carried out in the design phase.

Figures 6.30 and 6.31 show the next level down in the models and are used as a basis for one of the exercises at the end of the chapter, hence they are not described in any detail.

Figure 6.30 shows another process structure view, this time with the emphasis on the 'Component' element in the process model.

147

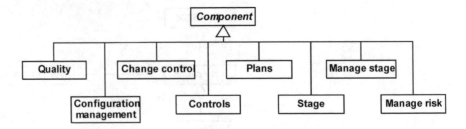

FIGURE 6.30 *Process structure view for Prince II, with an emphasis on 'Component'*

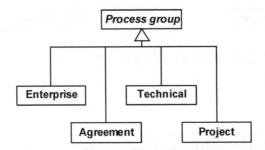

FIGURE 6.31 *Process structure view for ISO 15288, with an emphasis on 'Process group'*

Figure 6.31 shows the process structure view for ISO 15288, with an emphasis on 'Process group'.

CONCLUSIONS

This final chapter presented a case study that uses all of the techniques described in this book. The main aim has been to demonstrate how a complete process model may be developed. Although not fully populated, enough of the model has been completed to illustrate all the main concepts and ideas presented in the book. Also, the areas that have not been fully covered in this case study form the basis for a number of exercises in the next section.

EXERCISES

The following set of exercises have been specially designed to apply all the techniques employed in this book. There are two reasons for this. The obvious one is to enable you to test your knowledge and understanding of this book. The second reason is a bit more subtle, as carrying out these exercises will increase your confidence in both the approach and your own abilities before employing them 'in anger' in the real world.

1. Extend the process structure view to include the concepts of skills and responsibilities introduced in Figure 6.15.

2. Check the consistency between the process behaviour view in Figure 6.27 and the process content view in Figure 6.3.

3. Extend the mapping exercise to include the elements in Figures 6.30 and 6.31.

4. Update the requirements view in Figure 6.16 to include more detailed relationships between the requirements.

5. Add the following roles to the stakeholder view: 'Sales person', 'Marketer' and 'Sales manager'. In which grouping will they appear?

6. Increase the number of artefacts in the information view in Figure 6.21.

7. Populate some of the existing processes in the process content views shown in Figures 6.3 to 6.10.

8. Add some new processes to the process content view to reflect marketing-related processes.

9. Add some new instances of stakeholders to the process information views in Figures 6.22 and 6.23. Ensure consistency with the original requirements view.

10. Create a new process instance view diagram for any of the requirements in Figures 6.16 or 6.18.

11. Modify the process realization view of the existing process meta-model to include instances of stakeholders under the process instance view.

12. Create a process behaviour view for any of the processes in the process content views in Figures 6.3 to 6.10.

13. Define a process quagmire for the two process models introduced in Figures 6.28 and 6.29. Add some new source processes to the quagmire.

14. Consider the requirements view in Figure 6.17. What are the implications of moving the '<<extends>>' relationship, which currently exists between 'Cancel course' and 'Publicize', to between 'Cancel course' and 'Organize course'?

A Summary of the Process Modelling Meta-model

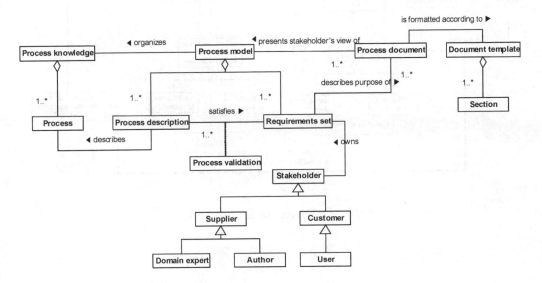

FIGURE A.1 *Process concept view*

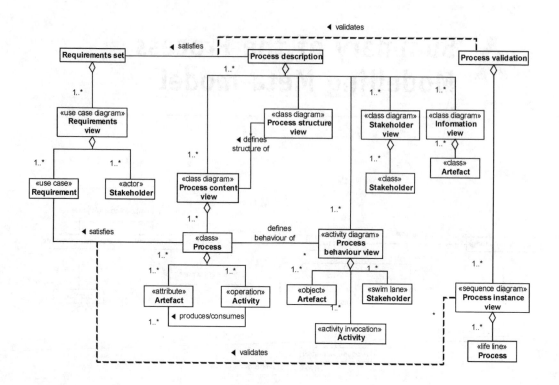

FIGURE A.2 *Process realization view*

B Summary of UML Notation

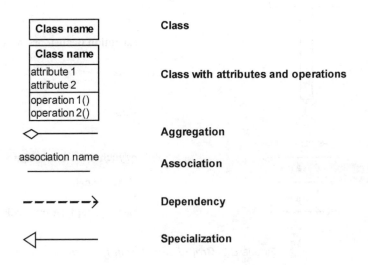

Class

Class with attributes and operations

Aggregation

Association

Dependency

Specialization

FIGURE B.1 *Graphical notation for class diagrams*

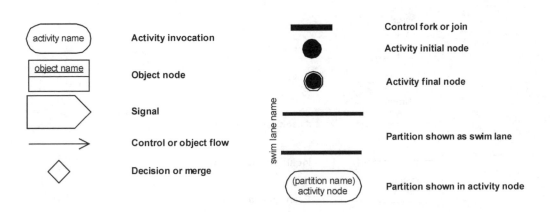

FIGURE B.2 *Graphical notation for activity diagrams*

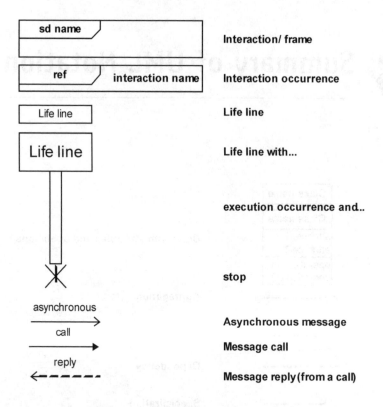

sd name	**Interaction/ frame**
ref interaction name	**Interaction occurrence**
Life line	**Life line**
Life line	**Life line with...**
	execution occurrence and..
	stop
asynchronous	**Asynchronous message**
call	**Message call**
reply	**Message reply (from a call)**

FIGURE B.3 *Graphical notation for sequence diagrams*

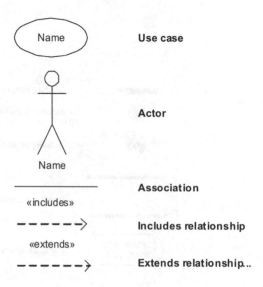

Name	**Use case**
	Actor
Name	
	Association
«includes»	**Includes relationship**
«extends»	**Extends relationship...**

FIGURE B.4 *Graphical notation for use case diagrams*

References

Bentley, C. (2001) *PRINCE 2: A practical handbook. Computer Weekly* Professional Series. Butterman Heineman, Oxford.

BPMI (2002) *Business Process Modelling Language.* BPMI, California. Available from www.bpmi.org.

Brooks, Frederick P. Jr (1995) *The Mythical Man-Month: Essays on Software.* Addison-Wesley, Reading, MA.

Cabinet Office (2004) *eGIF: The electronic government interoperability framework.* UK Government, London. Available from www.govtalk. gov.uk.

Carnegie Mellon Software Engineering Institute (2002) *Capability maturity model integration, version 1.1.* Carnegie Mellon Software Engineering Institute, Pittsburgh, PA. Available from www.sei.cmu.edu/cmmi.

Flowers, S. (1996) *Software Failure: Management Failure – Amazing stories and cautionary tales.* Wiley, Chichester.

Holt, J. (2004) *UML for Systems Engineering: Watching the wheels,* 2nd edition. IEE Publishing, London.

ISO 9001 (2000) *Model for quality assurance in design, development, production, installation and servicing.* ISO, Geneva.

ISO 12207 (2004) *Information technology: Software life cycle processes.* ISO, Geneva.

ISO 15288 (2002) *Systems engineering: System life cycle processes.* ISO, Geneva.

ISO 19501 (2005) *The unified modelling language.* ISO, Geneva.

ISO/IEC 15504 (2004) *Software process assessment.* ISO, Geneva.

Mazza, C., Fairclough, J., Melton, B., De Pablo, D., Scheffer, A. and Stevens, R. (1994) *Software Engineering Standards.* Prentice Hall, Hemel Hempstead.

Oxford English Dictionary (2002) ed. C. Soanes. Oxford University Press, Oxford.

Rumbaugh, J., Booch, G. and Jacobson, I. (2004) *The UML 2.0 Reference Manual.* Addison Wesley, Massachusetts.

Further Reading

ISO 90003 (2004) *Software engineering – Guidelines for the application of ISO 9001:2000 to computer software.* ISO, Geneva.

Slack, N., Chambers, S. and Johnston, R. (1998) *Operations Management.* London: FT Prentice Hall.

Index